DITCH THE DIET AND THE BUDGET

...and Find a Better Way to Live

CYNTHIA YATES

HARVEST HOUSE PUBLISHERS

EUGENE, OREGON

Cover by Terry Dugan Design, Minneapolis, Minnesota

Published in association with the literary agency of Janet Kobobel Grant, Books & Such, 4788 Carissa Avenue, Santa Rosa, California 95405

This book is not intended to take the place of sound professional financial or medical advice. Neither the author nor the publisher assumes any liability for possible adverse consequences as a result of the information contained herein.

DITCH THE DIET AND THE BUDGET...AND FIND A BETTER WAY TO LIVE
Copyright © 2004 by Cynthia Yates
Published by Harvest House Publishers
Eugene, Oregon 97402
www.harvesthousepublishers.com

Library of Congress Cataloging-in-Publication Data

Yates, Cynthia, 1947-
Ditch the diet and the budget—and find a better way to live / Cynthia Yates.
    p. cm.
ISBN 0-7369-1460-9 (pbk.)
1. Christian women—Religious life. 2. Finance, Personal—Religious aspects—Christianity. 3. Body image in women—Religious aspects—Christianity. I. Title.
BV4527.Y38 2004
248.8'43—dc22   2004004442

Printed in the United States of America

04 05 06 07 08 09 10 11 /VP-KB/ 10 9 8 7 6 5 4 3 2 1

I dedicate this book to my sisters,
Sheila and Anne,
two remarkable women whom I love and admire.
How I regret the times we've drifted apart!
How I cherish every moment we spend together!

Acknowledgments

Getting a book into print is a complex undertaking that involves far, far more people than the author. An entire battalion of knowledgeable folk stands behind each book, and I want to acknowledge them.

I want to acknowledge Servant Publications for publishing my first three books, and Broadman & Holman for publishing my novel. I want to acknowledge my friend and agent, Janet Kobobel Grant. And I want to acknowledge Harvest House. The professionals at Harvest House Publishers have gathered me into their experienced arms and guided me. The executives, the editors, the marketers, the administrators, and the tireless staff in publicity are the engine behind my latest books. I feel honored to be counted among their ranks.

Contents

A Note to the Reader...

I deliberately packed a lot into this book. Think of it as two books in one. Cramming information into a book is my style. I want to give you more than you expected—maybe 50 percent more.

Using humor, my own experience, and even a little sass, I also want to encourage you to think more deeply about issues that matter to you.

And that is what this book is—my attempt to bring the issues of body image and financial management to a deeper level, a next level, an "I never thought of it that way" level.

Writing a book that considers not only philosophical and spiritual realities of life but also plumbing and shopping—and the merits of pectin in apples—is challenging. And that is why I'm including this note to you.

If I was flinging a white-banded rock over my shoulder with my eyes shut tight right now (you'll read about that in chapter 5), I would be wishing this:

That you will read this book with pen in hand, notebook at the ready. That these pages will be dog-eared, smudged, underlined, bookmarked, laughed over, spilled on, and stained with curry (you'll read about that too). That they will cause you to reflect and to connect the dots, and that they will play a part, however small, in helping you to find—and to live—a much better life.

Part One

The Why
of It and the
Whole of It

Stop the ride; I want to get off. Take me to a place where I am not a slave to this maniacal push for perfection, where I accept who I am and am content with how I look and how much money I have.

ॐ   ॐ   ॐ

Perfection? Hah! I'd just like to make ends meet and finally squeeze into that cute little number that has become one with my closet. You know, the one with the permanent hanger marks in the shoulders…

1
A Mug of Tea, and You and Me

I didn't always have clean closets. Or a reasonably healthy body. Or a responsible plan for my financial future.

I didn't always have money squirreled under my mattress or sensible food stored in my cupboards. (Having a steady supply of Rocky Road ice cream or a stash of good, dark chocolate makes perfect sense.)

I didn't always pay my bills on time or eat just about anything I please. Or live an organized life. Or brag about low cholesterol.

In other words, I didn't always have a clue.

How I wish I'd had the good sense to read a book or two like this along the way—books that may have helped avert a lot of heartache. But no, not independent know-it-all me. I thought a budget seemed utterly unnecessary and spent fruitless years working toward an advanced degree in diet mania. I avoided the discipline of reasoned money management and kept my eyes peeled for that illusive quick fix that would turn me into a ravishing beach beauty. After all, I was in control and quite capable to chart my own course, thank you very much.

Yet when I look back, I don't see myself in the driver's seat at all, even though I acted cocky and self-assured. I was Ms. Clueless Person hitchhiking recklessly along a road to ruin. Life happened to me and I let it. I was along for the ride—not behind the wheel, not navigating from the passenger seat, not even a backseat driver. I was clinging to the car's back bumper, flapping in the wind, bloodied and bruised.

Certainly not a picture of the person who now exhorts others to practice sound stewardship, as I do on television and radio, or who stands in front of crowds as "Frugal Woman Extraordinaire." (Still working toward that ravishing beach beauty part.) So how did I get to this point? And what do clean closets have to do with budgets and diets, anyway? (Plenty.)

For one thing, the rides I hitched have taught me hard lessons with every turn, bump, and pothole. I've been dumped off at the side of the road and have tumbled into a pit of debt more times than I care to count. I've clawed my way back to the top, only to sabotage myself again (or be sabotaged by others), and there I went with a *splat*, slip-sliding back down again. Only through determination, some major attitude adjustment, scriptural imperative, and prayer have I broken free from the gut-wrenching bondage that money woes bring.

Will I ever be so free from concern over finances that I can throw caution to the wind? Never. Stewardship demands vigilance.

> *The Christian's primary stewardship is that of the gospel and includes the use of his whole life as well as his money.*
>
> F.L. FISHER

And the weight issue? Oh brudder. The only time I was thin was when I passed it on my way up the scale. I've bought the diet books and tried the foolproof plans. (I was the only "fool," as one "miracle" weight cure after another ended in failure.) I've joined the clubs and counted the numbers, all the while protesting that *I* don't follow diet trends. Yet my body seemed to stay the same, packing on a few extra pounds each year for good measure. As with my finances, only through determination, major attitude adjustment, scriptural imperative, and prayer have I managed to finally get the upper hand on this body of mine, inching my way toward a state of better health and fitness. I've reconciled that I will probably never be that ravishing beach beauty or shimmy into one of those thong things to swoon my way into Wonder Man's arms. (Husband Joe.)

Note from Joe: *Whew!*

Will I ever be able to let down my guard when it comes to body care? Never. Whether with budget or diet, stewardship demands vigilance.

Wait a minute! The title of this book tells me to ditch *diets and budgets—is this some kind of tricky bait and switch?*

Not at all. I am convinced that once I share what I have learned as I bounced along, you will be equipped to do just that—to ditch the demands, pressures, and guilt that come from your unrelenting quest. You will be able to resist the popular culture that insists that you follow its prescription for perfection and backs its demands with unlimited methodologies and how-tos for everything under the sun.

(Sun: that warm, golden, round thing in the sky that you used to take time to romp under, garden under, and laze, swim, and picnic under.)

Like many of you, I've learned a lot of how-tos during my life. I've even written books and articles on that level: how to save, how to shop, how to control the money monster, how to live well on any income, how to cut back on fat (try red licorice), how to cut back on sugar (sugar-free red licorice), how to cut back on chemicals (herb-flavored red licorice).

Note from me: *Yech!*

But…Why?

Before we address the how-tos, perhaps we should ask why. Do this, do that, tithe 10 percent, save 10 percent, fold it this way, use that coupon, bend over, walk three miles, eat more broccoli, breathe in deeply…*why?*

To lose weight and to save money, right? Sure…but why? What is the motivation behind this crazy push of ours?

❀ To be able to shop till you drop and look good in the latest midriff-baring, stiletto-wearing getup? Pul-leeze.

❀ Um…to carry a fat balance in your checking account and be able to eat anything you wish while wearing size-eight pedal pushers? Go deeper.

❀ Aha! To provide for retirement and be fit enough to enjoy those dandy golden years? Deeper.

❀ Got it! To be able to use money and possessions for the betterment of others and for your own improved health so you don't ultimately burden others? Deeper still.

Why we strive toward financial stability and svelte bodies is a complex question with complex answers. We just saw that answers can start shallow and get deeper. Together we will fish in deep waters as we consider why as well as how-to. Make no mistake: How-tos are important. They are why you bought this book in the first place.

I just want to put the horse before the cart. I'll start by introducing you to a couple of my family members.

My Unconventional Sister

I have a sister named Sheila who, as far as I am concerned, is certifiably daft. A half-bubble off plumb. Ahead of her time. Annoying as all get-out. She is also one of the kindest and most intelligent persons I know, and I love her to death.

Now, because I am regarded in my family as…well, the *pudgy* one, one of my two sisters (my other sister is Anne) or my mother will commonly make casual reference to such things as dietary constraint, genetic abnormality ("What planet did *you* drop down from? No one else in our gene pool has short, hairy legs and such a huge posterior."), or the fact that I must sit for extended periods of time on said posterior in order to write, such as I am doing now. Have you ever tried penning your novel on a treadmill?

Mom: "You *sit* too much—what do you expect? You should wear slimming clothes. Get a big blouse that covers your rear. And while you're at it, make sure it's striped vertically. And color! *Sheesh,* Cynthia! You *never* wear color! And I read that you should wear pretty scarves to bring attention upward. You have *such* a pretty face."

All of this is vexing.

Anyway, Sheila called me one morning, positively breathless, and announced with utmost authority why I wasn't successful with my latest diet regimen. (Knowing it all *is* in our gene pool.)

Sheila: "Iknowwhyyou'renotlosingweight!" (Sheila talks like this—one continuous sentence without punctuation.)

Me: (Scratching abundant posterior and peering at my bedside clock:) "Sheil, it's six A.M."

Sheila: "I just read something that's going to *change your life* and make you successful and you're not only going to lose weight but have record book sales and your love life will blossom and I'm coming right over."

Me: (Looking over my shoulder at Wonder Man, snoring next to me:) "Sheil, it's six A.M."

Sheila: "This is the answer to *everything!* It's all the rage in Bulgaria—or is it Des Moines? I forget."

Me: (Always eager to improve my love life:) "So why don't you come over for lunch…Sheil? Sheil?"

Sheila was on her way. One hour later we were rearranging the furniture in my living room.

Sheila: *"Furniture placement,* Cynthia. That's the key! Your living room is all wrong. You need to move all this stuff around so the energy can flow freely. Help me move this floor plant toward the entrance. Too much energy is not good either. I know these things; I read a lot. You'll be thin in no time."

> Trust in the LORD with all your heart
> and lean not on your own understanding;
> in all your ways acknowledge him,
> and he will make your paths straight.
>
> PROVERBS 3:5-6

So I moved the plant. And the sofa. And the coffee table. I was aware of the philosophical premise of the *feng shui* principles Sheila was promoting, and as a biblical Christian, I know I must be careful where I put my trust. I mean, to me it's a no-brainer: trust my furniture or trust God. Gee, let me see...

I moved the sofa just the same and went along with my sister out of respect for her earnest concern toward me. Besides, my living room *was* a bit cluttered.

Turns out Sheila had a point.

Our living room *didn't* "flow." Furniture blocked vital pathways to make physical movement within the room—and enjoyment of the room—complicated. Once we rearranged the furniture, the room was much more inviting, felt better, and actually looked better. All from repositioning what I already had.

You see, I didn't have to add to what I had to make my living room "work." I already had the furniture I needed. Probably more than I needed. I just needed to step back and consider different placement strategies and different emphasis of certain pieces.

You too already have everything you need to live a better life, especially if weight control and finance seem complicated to you. You already know you're supposed to pare down to a healthy weight and live within your means. To be utterly blunt, you even already know how. But you just can't seem to turn it all around, can you? At least not in any lasting manner. I know. I'm not a whole lot different from you—just a step or two ahead of you, that's all.

Live Better

Would you like to feel better—to live better?

Do you live life with a nagging sense of dissatisfaction? Do you chart your path only to trip over an ill-placed coffee table? Are your plans foiled as if someone rolled a heavy bookcase in your way? Are you trapped in a maze of frustrating activity and push, as if stuck in a room with vital pathways to joy and accomplishment blocked with clutter? Do you feel as if your body is turning into the Blob That Ate Detroit? Are you angry with yourself for your "I give up" attitude about getting back into shape?

Welcome to the world of being fully human, just like the rest of us. You may feel as if you're on a sinking ship, but I'd wager that if you checked the closest lifeboat you'd find that it's crammed to the gunwales with other people just like you. People who need an early morning wake-up call and an offer to rearrange their living rooms to get rid of some clutter.

This book will certainly take a look at your living room—and your bedroom and your garage and your kitchen cupboard—as I offer dozens of suggestions that will help you toward much greater fiscal responsibility and, I sincerely hope, a more fit body. That is the how. My aim is to help you toward such efficiency and know-how that responsible finance and weight control become the automatic results of the wise use of your...shall we say... energy.

To be really honest means...making
confession whether you can afford it or not;
refusing unmerited praise; looking
painful truths in the face.

AUBREY DE VERE

We will also look at a couple of rooms you carry along with you wherever you go, a couple of rooms that may have had furniture in place for so long that the carpet is permanently dented and the paint has faded. The rooms may be filled with dust or cobwebs, and furniture may be too broken or too shabby to be of any use. Or perhaps you merely need to bring these rooms into the twenty-first century by adding a bit of zip or pizzazz. You may be ready for change.

Carpet dents? Ice cubes are supposed to work wonders.

The rooms I'm talking about are in your mind and in your heart. How long has it been since you've rearranged the furniture there?

I thought this book was about ditching...

Hold your horses.

I believe success starts in your mind and in your heart. Visit those rooms. Sit down and look around. Are the doors locked? Blast your way in if need be. This is where you go to honestly find out why you do what you do, whether it is destructive or productive. This is also where you go to find the fortitude and determination to proceed and to succeed. Only when your mind and heart are without clutter (transformed) can you successfully reposition real furniture in any room of your house.

My Son the Doctor

Wonder Man and I have one child—a man, now—our son, Joshua. Josh is married and has graced us with grandchildren. At this writing, he is close to becoming a Doctor of Sociology. I admire and respect Joshua for his perseverance and accomplishment. I have learned much from him, if only by association.

How I wish I had Joshua's knowledge, his mind, his education! I would so like to write something profound, to be one of those experts who appear on C-SPAN and speak with lofty language and dish out statistics like lifesavers. Or to sit in a mahogany-lined study and discuss the finer points of the economy over a dainty teacup of Earl Grey. But no can do.

My education came from the School of Hard Knocks. I didn't graduate from the University of Anyplace. I have been down (and nearly out) and so broke that a gallon of superglue might not have put me back together. I have been a single mom, I have been homeless, and I have been penniless. I have even contemplated ending my life when no hope was in sight. (Didn't bother to think *that* out.) And the body issue? I can still hardly look into a mirror or glance at a store window. I've been fighting the pudgy-to-fat predicament all of my life.

The best I can do is to leave the lofty language to others and join you at your kitchen table to guzzle Lipton from a chipped mug while discussing the finer points of making your mortgage payment. Or the merits of herb-flavored licorice.

Teachers Along the Way

As I've learned how to live a better life, I've come to admire (or at least learn from) several people.

One fellow is named Wendell Berry. My Son the Doctor brought this prolific writer to my attention. Wendell Berry is a man with unwavering dedication to preserving the wholeness of family and community, "a human being speaking with calm and sanity out of the wilderness," according to the *Washington Post*.

Berry writes about stress, ill-health, and what he sees as the destructiveness of American culture. He knows the "why" and goes straight to the heart (and mind) of it. I would like to be like Wendell Berry.

We all know the domestic bliss types. These are women and men who have mastered the art of home-tending, cooking, gardening, building, and more. In other words, these people know what a monkey wrench is and how to use one. They turn out perfect soufflés (as if we make soufflés for dinner any more), pave their own driveways, and successfully grow houseplants. They appear on television regularly and highlight our ineptitude (as if we need reminding). I would like to be like these types, though my home-tending occasionally lines up more with Moe, Larry, and Curly. (Especially when I'm facing a book deadline.)

You're undoubtedly familiar with the late Erma Bombeck. Erma had a funny way with words that helped us to laugh at ourselves. Her newspaper columns resonated with us as she recounted her resolve to finally decode the remote for the VCR, extract a CD from its case, or harvest penicillin from cheese mold growing in her fridge.

We all liked Erma because Erma was like all of us. Her humor gave us commonality with each other. In her own way, Erma built community. When we read Erma Bombeck's column, we became part of a clear majority of stressed, imperfect, pudgy—and fully human—neighbors. I would like to be like Erma.

You're probably not familiar with my other sister, Anne. Annie is not only brilliant and resourceful but also a fitness buff. You know the kind—she can knit a tent with her teeth while pedaling up Mt. Rushmore with fresh bread baking on her bike's back bumper. Annie is trim, trim, trim. She can lift a '57 Pontiac with her pinky, leap over a huddle of sleeping dogs on her kitchen floor, and run several thousand miles each day before work. In the dark. Over boulders. With cement blocks strapped to her feet. Backward.

Insofar as the fitness thing is concerned, I am *nothing* like my sister Anne, whom I also love to death.

Those are a few people whom I admire or have learned from. There is One, however, whom I try hardest to emulate, to copy, to follow. He is the *only* One who could transform this know-it-all's mind, heart, and life immeasurably and permanently. Hand in hand with Christ, I began to tentatively walk through the locked doors of my mind and heart, and in Christ I continually strive to find my identity.

> *I have come upon the happy discovery that this life hid with Christ in God is a continuous unfolding.*
>
> EUGENIA PRICE

We have much to learn from the words and life of Jesus. When I read His words, I am motivated, hopeful, happy, shamed, determined, and eternally grateful. I can only hope and pray that when I depart this life, others will think of me as a person who was a tiny bit like Jesus. That, to me, will have been a life well lived. A better life, indeed.

These people have helped me learn to be content with life, to ditch diet and budget cares by converting them from exacting duty to simple second nature. They have helped me learn to celebrate the abundance of my blessings. And they have shown me that living well, living a better life, has nothing to do with body image or money. Rather, it's about living according to God's purpose for my life, recognizing that regardless of my circumstance, He is in control. It's about the joy that reality brings, even in the face of hardship or adversity. If I strive toward perfection in anything, it is that.

And now it's time for us to have a chat. I hope that by the time our conversation is over, you too will be able to ditch your diet and your budget and to simply live a better, more calmly efficient and Christ-driven life.

The Tale of a Bad Day

The alarm went off 15 minutes ago. You are too comfortable to move. Your mind kicks into gear: If you cut time from your shower and eat on the fly (or don't eat at all—you *are* trying to lose weight), you can coax another 15 minutes into your slumber. Fifteen turns into 20, forcing you to go from 0 to 60. You fling the blankets back and hit the floor with a thud, pausing long enough to wonder if your morning dash qualifies for aerobic activity. After all, you have jolted your heart—along with the rest of your body—as you bounded from bed.

Sounds of *Clifford the Big Red Dog* inform you that Junior is already camped in front of PBS Kids. A rap on Missy's door begins the ugly morning ritual of dragging her from bed; her sister wakes up loud and clear with a wail from her crib, diaper no doubt sodden because of the long draft from her sippy cup late last night.

"Mommy will be right there, Precious," you call, as Missy feigns a comatose state. You need coffee. Once again, Hubby-Dearest has left for his morning jog without starting the coffeemaker, and this monumental act of disregard for your needs sets you off as sure as that alarm clock. Groping around the kitchen, you find the jar of coffee beans is empty, but yesterday's coffee (and filter and grounds) is full. As you tend to this, the soggy filter rips, depositing old coffee grounds on the bottom of an already mildewed filter tray. Yum. Junior shouts from the TV room for his favorite cereal. Precious is now up to a shriek, and Missy remains comatose.

Once you've emptied an entire kitchen cupboard to find more beans and the coffee is brewing, you pick up your pace. As you barge toward the demanding wail, you make a few demands yourself: "Get up! This is the last time I'm going to tell you!"

Junior drops a dozen eggs on the floor as he raids the fridge for milk for his cereal—the cereal box, after all, now within easy reach on the counter from your coffee bean search. Not to worry: Barky the cocker spaniel to the rescue.

Diaper changed, Precious gets deposited on the bathroom floor to play with assorted towels, toys, pot lids, and clothes while you hop into the shower, screaming at Missy, who finally materializes in the bathroom door with a demand of her own: "I've got to go. Now!"

To be continued...

2
The Impossible Dream

Resolution: *a mental pledge, something
one intends to do*

Revolution: *substitution of a new system...
especially by force*

OXFORD AMERICAN DICTIONARY

Diet and Budget. Add flossing teeth and you have the holy grail of New Year's resolutions. The trouble is, we have yet to learn we need a *revolution* to finally achieve these goals. Merchandisers salivate in anticipation of our annual January ritual. Television ads appear like clockwork, hawking "get slim quick" formulas that the latest celebrities promise will help you lose a gazillion pounds. Budget balancers hit bookstores with a vengeance.

(Not to be left out, a newfangled toothpaste appears on the scene with floss built into its cap, which we all know will be *real* appealing considering the goopy mess that usually accumulates up there.)

We buy sweat pants, pedometers, storage bins, and computer programs, and we sharpen our pencils with zeal. This year is going to be different! New leaf time! Set the alarm clock! Turn down the thermostat! We're going to live within our means! Drink more water! Eat an apple a day! Sugar be banned!

Brown bags appear as a sure sign of our more frugal and healthier lunch habits, and we earnestly equip our shiny new lockers at the shiny new athletic club with chamomile-laced body cream, organic shampoos, and loofahs. We are on a roll. And in the midst of it all—yes, even before we go *splat* against the gymnasium wall, we lose touch with simply living. Our time, energy, and money have gone toward the latest method, protocol, or pledge to reach dietary or budgetary goals—goals which seem to become increasingly unreachable.

(If you are anything like me in years past, within a few days of your dietary resolve you're ripping open a bag of potato chips with your car keys before you hit the grocery store parking lot.)

The purpose of this book is to demonstrate that by catching your breath and simply living, you can set realistic and therefore reachable goals. I want to coax you toward *contentment within your circumstance* without becoming unrealistic or nostalgic—and without abandoning the message that most of us should manage our bodies and our money more effectively. Once we appraise this maniacal cultural drive of ours, we will see that if it brought us success in the first place, we would not be in hot eternal pursuit.

Think of it this way: You've been handling money and reading money-saving tips all of your adult life—so how come you are in debt up to your eyeballs? You've been dieting in some manner all of your adult life—so how come you're not thin as a thermometer?

We live meanly, like ants; though fable tells us
that we were long ago changed into men...it is error
upon error, and clout upon clout, and our best
virtue has for its occasion a superfluous
and evitable wretchedness.

HENRY DAVID THOREAU

How Did We Get on This Treadmill?

This is where I need the insight of our son and his cohorts. Call me an amateur sociologist by association, not because of Joshua but because I've been reading about, watching, and participating in social trends for nearly 60 years. (Ouch! That hurt!) I have my suspicions about how we ended up in this frenzied quest for more stuff (material goods) and less stuffing (weight control).

We live in an advanced industrial society at the beginning of the twenty-first century. Nary a day goes by that we aren't delighted and captivated by new advances in science and technology, many of them beneficial. Along with our captivation comes an incessant drumbeat through ads and commercials that we must have that latest technological gadget or gizmo in order to complete our lives. (Or the latest model of a Chevrolet pickup truck, Wonder Man.) We can't sit on public transportation, go to school, watch a ball game, or look at our home computer without being sold to and pandered to (*panhandled* is more like it). And the enticements are slick, designed to create desire, need, and want. Add to this the easy credit that comes knocking on our door. Credit, I might add, that lenders offer to us without the slightest interest in our ability to repay.

Interest—that's the trap. From this day forward, think of interest as quicksand. And think of credit cards as *debt* cards, because credit card accounts are *designed* to keep you in debt. If you doubt me, read the fine print on your contracts. Ah...you don't even have that skinny, folded-up contract that came with the card? Just as I said: fully human.

So what do we have so far? Advanced industrial society. Technology. Seductive advertising. Easy credit.

Now add unspoken new standards, fostered in part by our buddies down on Madison Avenue—standards that have elbowed their way to the front of the line, shoving once-ingrained virtues of thrift and care and self-control out the back door. Here are two of the new standards: Life is never good enough, and everything is disposable. The incessant message that we must be new and improved fosters dissatisfaction. To my recollection, the idea of disposable products started years ago with men's razors. Now people nonchalantly *expect* to replace their possessions regularly either because of poor workmanship, that new technology I mentioned, or the constant need for change. These days *disposable* is an accepted term for anything from cameras to televisions, and we think nothing of throwing things away from sheer boredom.

Advanced industrial society. Technology. Seductive advertising. Easy credit. Dissatisfaction. Disposable. Let's throw into the mix the very real issue of genetics or physiological predispositions, as well as social conditioning. That's enough right there. But I am not the type to leave well enough alone.

We need to factor in some rather unpleasant yet common flaws of our human condition: sin. Whoopsie... did I just lose you? Don't go yet! Stick around and hear what God has to say.

Thumbing through my fat theological dictionary, I came across what are commonly called the "seven deadly sins." That sounded ominous. The list basically represents major categories, or primary human instincts, that are most likely to give rise to sin. What's on the list? Pride, covetousness, lust, envy, gluttony, anger, and sloth.

Either God or sin must die in my life.

Let's explore this list to see how primary a role each item plays in our incessant drive for more. (I'm also curious to know where I stand in the lineup!)

Pride: an attempt to appear in a superior light. (Oops. Been fighting this one for a long, long time.) Pride, according to G.B. Stanton, is the parent of discontent, ingratitude, presumption, passion, extravagance, and bigotry. We all know God opposes the proud (James 4:6).

Covetousness: L.T. Corlett says the word means "inordinate desire," especially in the realm of material things. Covetousness (or greed) is labeled idolatry (Colossians 3:5) because the intensity of desire and worship are closely related. Jesus sternly warned against this: "greed, malice, deceit, lewdness, envy, slander, arrogance and folly. All these evils come from inside and make a man 'unclean' " (Mark 7:22).

Lust: desire and longing. In sinful man, desire becomes inordinate, or our desires do not follow God's will for our lives. In John's summary statement of sin, he says this: "For everything in the world—the cravings of sinful man, the lust of his eyes and the boasting of what he has and does—comes not from the Father but from the world" (1 John 2:16). And who can forget Paul's well-quoted verse: "For the love of money is a root of all kinds of evil" (1 Timothy 6:10).

> Lust is an appetite by which temporal goods are preferred to eternal goods.
> AUGUSTINE

Envy: Envy is just plumb bad. The most telling biblical example is its ruinous and deadly effect upon Saul, whose envy of David "did more to break his health than his advancing years" (R. McCracken). (Does wishing I looked like one of those ravishing beach beauties count?)

Gluttony: (I held my fingers over my eyes as I investigated this one, lover of food that I am.) Proverbs tells us to put a knife to our throats if we are given to gluttony (23:2) and warns

that drunkards and gluttons become poor (23:21). In Philip-
pians, Paul's epistle of joy, he writes, "Their destiny is destruc-
tion, their god is their stomach, and their glory is in their
shame. Their mind is on earthly things" (3:19). Sobering.

Anger: What could anger have to do with this consumptive,
never satisfied, driven society of ours? We might be quick to
mention *God's* anger toward our apparent greed. But what
about us? What about our anger? Proverbs 14:17 offers sage
warning: "A quick-tempered man does foolish things." But I
was looking for something more useful for this book. I found it
in the short New Testament book of Titus: "Since an overseer
is entrusted with God's work, he must be blameless—not over-
bearing, not quick-tempered, not given to drunkenness, not
violent, not pursuing dishonest gain" (1:7). Who are the over-
seers entrusted to God's work? We are.

Sloth: Proverbs 24:30 says it well: "I went past the field of
the sluggard, past the vineyard of the man who lacks judgment;
thorns had come up everywhere, the ground was covered with
weeds, and the stone wall was in ruins." (That sounds like my
garden at times!)

Alrighty then. Kind of convincing and convicting, isn't it? I
will leave the matter of sin and the controversy that surrounds
sin to others. But I know a couple things for sure:

1. Sin alienates us from God because He is holy.

2. Christ reunites us.

I have learned something else about sin: It can be personal
or social, individual or collective. "It is through regeneration by
the Spirit, the imparting of faith and love," says D.G. Bloesch,
"that the sinner is set free from bondage to sin and enabled to
achieve victory over sin in everyday life." Or, as a little girl
once said, repentance means being sorry enough to quit. An

ever vigilant and prayerful person remains aware of the threat of sin's bondage.

Advanced industrial society, technology, seductive advertising, easy credit, dissatisfaction, disposable goods, physiology, social imperatives, and sin—these are some of the fundamental aspects of our unsettled lives. (Advances in industry and technology can be very helpful, but they can also contribute to our lack of focus and direction.) Now we turn to the essential theme of this book: our bondage to society's impossible demands.

The Impossible Dream

Man of La Mancha hit Broadway in the '60s. In that smash musical, the protagonist, Don Quixote, sings a showstopper— "The Impossible Dream."

He sings about his dream, his glorious quest. On and on he croons about his apparent determination to chase his dream— an illusion—all the way to Mars, if need be, as he reaches for "the unreachable star." He traipses all over Spain, Sancho Panza in tow, captivating and infuriating people with his missionary zeal. And he tilts a couple of windmills in the process.

No offense intended for those of us who embraced those sentiments (I knew the score by heart), but the guy rode through life on a bony pony and died on a cold dungeon floor. Yippee skippee. Was Don Quixote's "ride into hell for a heavenly cause" a noble quest? Yessireebob. But you know—someone already did that for us.

I bring this lovable fellow from La Mancha to our attention to illustrate how easily we can tilt windmills as we push forward, our impossible dreams just a step ahead of us. "New and improved" is just around the corner, but when we get around that corner, yet another "new and improved" taunts us.

Okay, comparing that sweet old man's virtuous quest to our cultural march toward our own illusive and unreachable "stars" may be a bit of a stretch. But just think about Don Quixote's language for a moment: impossible, unreachable, quest, hopeless. Sooner or later we're going to get sore bums from riding that bony critter. *There's* a fulfilling and fun life. Got a sidecar on that pony?

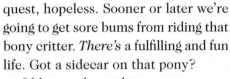

Attitudes are shaped by worldview. Is your worldview shaped by popular culture or by the love of God? In other words, for whom do you live?

I like my dream better.

Understand—I would no more promote a hedonistic live-for-the-moment lifestyle than I would demean sentiment or hard work. Neither would I suggest for a *second* that we are entitled to some sort of materialistic prosperity or life of leisure as God's children. The whole entitlement thing is part of the reason many of us are in the physical and financial predicaments we are in. More on that later.

My dream is pretty straightforward: *to live well—and contentedly—within my circumstance as a vital witness to a watching world.* Frankly, I believe that is my Christian responsibility and privilege.

The apostle Paul told Timothy that "godliness with contentment is great gain." Paul was talking about a proper perspective on and attitude toward life.

So where do we find this perspective? I can only tell you again where I found it: in the words and life of Jesus Christ—Emmanuel—God with us.

To the Greater Glory of God

Remember the *carpe diem* phase we went through a few years back? Seize the day! Live for today!

We appropriated that philosophy for a while. T-shirts, ball caps, and coffee mugs reminded us to smell the roses, to play, to lighten up. Frankly, for a stressed and driven society, that was an important message.

> *For I am convinced that neither death nor life, neither angels nor demons, neither the present nor the future, nor any powers, neither height nor depth, nor anything else in all creation, will be able to separate us from the love of God that is in Christ Jesus our Lord.*
>
> ROMANS 8:38

What seems more important to me, though, is to live today for the One who has so excellently blessed me. Should not our lives be *ad majorem Dei gloriam?* Live today all right, but live for the greater honor and glory of God.

Let me cut to the chase. Lots of swell people tap-dance around some "higher power" concept as if they would offend others (or their own sensibilities) by suggesting such a being as God exists. This, to me, is dumb. If there really *is* a God, is *their* sense of reasoning greater than His? Sure—and pigs fly.

If God is real—and I believe He is—we are talking *huge.* Beyondo. Way past our capacity to wrap our limited, finite brains around. Way higher than high.

So if this God not only made us but is the first cause, the source of everything, and consummate love, we're not talking about some sort of mean galactic extraterrestrial with a lightning bolt. We're talking about "the compassionate and gracious God, slow to anger, abounding in love and faithfulness, maintaining love to thousands, and forgiving wickedness, rebellion and sin" (Exodus 34:6-7).

Bring honor and glory to *that* God, and you will be able to answer the "why" question we asked in the first chapter.

When we fish in the deeper waters of our true motivations, we begin to find that a genuine reason to strive toward perfection is to honor God. And I believe one way we honor God is to live responsible and satisfied lives in the midst of our circumstance. That does not mean we should not work to improve our circumstance. Satisfaction with the moment does not mean resignation to dire, unprofitable, or hard times. It means the same thing now that it did nearly 2000 years ago when Paul wrote his first letter to the Thessalonians and told them to "give thanks in all circumstances, for this is God's will for you in Christ Jesus" (5:18).

The LORD will guide you always; he will satisfy your needs in a sun-scorched land and will strengthen your frame. You will be like a well-watered garden, like a spring whose waters never fail.

ISAIAH 58:11

Thank You, Lord

Thanksgiving both glorifies and honors God. The psalmist says that we are to praise God with song and glorify Him with thanksgiving, and that whoever gives thank offerings honors God.

Did you know that God requires thanksgiving of us? Give thanks to the Lord, let us be thankful, sing and make music, always give thanks. Christ gave thanks often. The Bible cites many reasons to thank God: for answered prayer, for Christian giving, for civil authorities, for converts, for faith and love, for the goodness of God, for the grace of Christ, for the inheritance of God's kingdom, for the presence of God, for rescue from sin, for the Word and works of God, for everything.

For what do you thank God? Listing the big stuff is easy: His Son, family, friends, health, your job, where you live, good fortune that's come your way. Those things are certainly key to us all. But consider the command to give thanks in everything. This is a small—but important—step toward a worldview overhaul if your cares are not now grounded in the grace and mercy of God.

Walk in creation as pilgrimage and give thanks.

Generously give thanks today. Give thanks for the wonder of creation, for daily bread, for families, for a mind to think and heart to love, for hands to serve, and for art and music and leisure.

Thank Him for the umpteenth interruption of a little child, for the rock-solid stability of your mate, for the dog beneath your feet. Thank Him for troubles that test your trust and instruct you. Thank Him for knowing your heart or for cupping that heart in His hands in time of sorrow.

Your daily thanksgiving will serve as a reminder to you of the good providence of the One in whom we delight and who delights in us. How does He delight in us? Listen to the prophet Zephaniah!

> The LORD, your God, is in your midst, a warrior who gives victory; he will rejoice over you with gladness, he will renew you in his love; he will exult over you with loud singing as on a day of festival (3:17-18 RSV).

God is not a grump! He ordained festivals. Take some time to leaf through the psalms. Look for words like clap, sing, shout, dance, and rejoice. And then give thanks.

Thank You (*Sob*) So Very Much

Or a different variation: "Thank you (*#!@#!) very much."
Doesn't work that way, does it? Unless overcome by emotion because of someone's generosity, or begrudgingly murmuring thanks through clenched teeth, thanksgiving is a joyful expression. It is heartfelt, earnest, happy, and often excited. "Thank you!" we exclaim with a smile.

> Give thanks and take time to celebrate life today. It's right under your nose.

With that in mind, we can easily see how giving thanks for everything—as we are told to do in the Word of God—will have a positive effect on our attitude. It will also be a continuous reminder of our blessings, regardless of our circumstance. And it will help us to be satisfied with that circumstance.

What's the flip side of thanks? Ingratitude. Ingratitude is a downright awful-sounding sentiment. I dare say that none of us want to be an ingrate toward God.

The flip side of thanks could also be "no thanks." Think about it.

The Flip Side

I've been toying with the notion of "flip sides" for a long time. What is the flip side of personality traits, of behavior, of likes, of dislikes? What happens when we turn them inside out?

Some things are obvious: The flip side of war is peace, the flip side of hate is love, the flip side of sorrow is happiness, the flip side of discontent is contentment.

What could be considered the flip side of our cultural imperative to push and shove our way toward a self-centered existence? It is the biblical imperative to obey and pray our way toward a Christ-centered existence.

In this chapter, I've explored factors that contribute to what I consider to be our cultural malaise. I've also explored the flip side of these trends: bringing honor and glory to God, being content within our circumstance, offering thanksgiving, and connecting to joy. We have seen the counsel, guidance, and command of Scripture—an answer to the question why. If, by going deeper, we have found that stewardship of our finances, our bodies — our lives—is motivated by an utter abandonment of ourselves to our love for God *and our identity found in Jesus Christ,* we will quit our obsession for worldly perfection, ditch unrealistic pursuits, and most certainly live a better life.

> "Thank you, Lord Jesus!" I utter that spontaneously. Out loud. Several times each day. Do I care who's listening? Nah.

A Word About Stewardship

What does *stewardship* actually mean, anyway? Well, it actually means "management of a household." At a broader level, the word has come to mean the "administration of duties or goods in one's care." The Bible starts right off the bat with clear instructions to us that we are to be God's stewards. We are entrusted not only with money and possessions but also with the gospel message.

A Prayer

Though I cannot decide upon a favorite book of the Bible, a favorite verse, or a favorite "formal" prayer, I hold one prayer particularly dear. It is a prayer of self-dedication that comes from *The Book of Common Prayer.* I share it with you now as an excellent act of commitment for you to pray daily.

Almighty and eternal God, so draw my heart to you, so guide my mind, so fill my imagination, so control my will, that I may be wholly yours, utterly dedicated to you; and then use me, I pray you, as you will, and always to your glory and to the welfare of your people; through our Lord and Savior Jesus Christ. Amen.

The Possible Dream

In the next chapter I will begin to outline specific principles that will guide you toward the better life you crave. Though I will continue to emphasize "why," I will offer practical steps and sensible goals. In other words, I'm going to begin the gradual shift to "how." How *do* you ditch that diet and budget, anyway?

The Tale of a Bad Day

No time to dry your hair. The towel it was wrapped in comes undone and hangs off your head like a terry goiter while you stuff Precious into an outfit she outgrew two months ago. You send the contents of her crammed dresser drawer flying as you search for matching socks.

Are we the only family on the planet that has to stop at Wal-Mart on the way to church, so the kids don't look entirely like the Clampetts?

Wet and steaming from his morning jog, your husband appears with freshly brewed coffee in his hands, which he drinks in front of you. Missy and Junior fight over the last clean spoon, and you settle the argument by washing a dirty spoon from the dishwasher, which you have to pry open using both feet and both hands due to haphazard jamming from pots, pans, baby bottles, and a rubber doll that burps.

At that moment you hear one of the most incredibly stupid questions in the history of mankind, a question that might be funny were it not for the fact that you are now homicidal: "Honey, could you iron a white shirt for me?"

Missy sits on a chair and stares at the wall, eyes glazed. Junior tracks sticky eggs throughout the house. Precious occupies herself at the dog dish (kibble is so much more appealing than zwieback). Barky mops up after everyone, her long ears trailing egg goo.

You begin to think about the day: Deposit kids (childcare, preschool, school), drop off dry cleaning and overdue DVDs, buy more eggs, call the vet to find out if Barky needs her stomach pumped from all those shells, call the groomer to get her a bath, call the lawyer to initiate a divorce (not really), and oh yeah, work. You feel guilty—again—about your decision to go back to work, but your goal to contribute financially to the household coffers is noble. You might finally be able to get control of your bills—and besides, *should* you be guilty doing something you like? You do everything in your power to nurture your children and hold all the pieces together. Work gives you a chance to use your education and to make a difference on a broader scale...

You touch your long hair. Still wet. Time ticks on. It should be dry by the 8:45 staff meeting. You remind yourself you need an overhead for your presentation. Ohmygosh! The presentation! You were going to get up early to finish...

To be continued...

3
Just DITCH It!

eople often wonder why diets and budgets fail again and
again despite sincere intentions and New Year's resolutions. I believe the reason is this: Many of us have failed to look
at our motivation (or lack thereof).

We have seen that the *primary* reason to control your body
weight (health) and your finances is that you are commanded
to by a holy God, and you *want* to honor Him because you
love Him. I'm guessing many of you are thinking, *Hmm—now
that you put it that way...*

The Whole of It: A Winning Team

I urge you to continue to readjust your perspective. A good
way to accomplish this is by thinking holistically. Many books
promote a holistic approach to health, but have you considered a holistic approach to financial health? Most people
haven't. So how do mind, body, and spirit combine to form a
winning team? Let's look at a new mind-set (mind), skill-set
(body), and heart-set (spirit).

We all need a healthy **mind-set.** That is the *will* to save or to
pare down our weight, the *decision* to face our situation head-on
(for the umpteenth time if necessary), and the *resolve* to get
through any predicament we might be in.

We also need a healthy **skill-set.** That is how we are going to
do what needs to be done. It includes the steps we can take, the

tricks we can learn to outwit our limited means or our battle of the bulge, and the strategies we can learn. Your skill-set is your practical knowledge and resourcefulness. It is here that so many of us lack training and simple common sense. Part 2 of this book tackles this aspect with gusto.

I have already urged you to dig a little more deeply and look at your **heart-set**—the spiritual imperative behind your overall stewardship. This gets at the question why.

> *Love the Lord your God with all your heart and with all your soul and with all your mind. This is the first and greatest commandment.*
>
> JESUS

Ready to Dig a Ditch? How About Five?

Now we come to the moment you may have been waiting for: We're going to DITCH your diet and your budget.

My method is fivefold. I'm hoping to equip you with a system that is as unforgettable as the title of this book. Your job is to remember the word "DITCH." Using it as an acronym, each letter will represent a vital action that will lead you toward habitual stewardship of body and money, which I believe will make better living automatic. The words are *deconstruct, information, try, consumption,* and *health.*

A budget is what you plan in advance to spend.

For the record, I am *not* against budgeting or dieting, if by budgeting we mean using a sensible plan for financial savings and disbursement, or if by dieting we mean following a sensible plan for health that includes a realistic weight goal. We can't succeed in life without a plan, folks.

Deconstruct

D stands for *deconstruct*. Body image and finances are two critical areas of your life. To deconstruct means to take apart your perspectives on your body image and your finances.

How have you looked at weight control and finances before now? What do you need to rethink? What thoughts do you need to conform to your beliefs or to your sincere intention to adopt a more biblical worldview? How do other people affect you? Hah! Never mind others—how do you affect yourself?

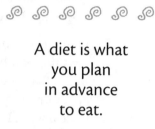

A diet is what
you plan
in advance
to eat.

Just Crazy Ol' You

I've written other books about the critical need to honestly appraise your financial situation (*not* to approximate it) if you want to work your way out of a hole. You start by courageously opening your mail and totaling your bills. Also, by determining your actual income.

This book goes to the next level of physical and financial health. If you sincerely want your love of God to underlie and motivate your stewardship effort, don't just open your mail—open your heart and mind and have a peek. Storm those dusty rooms in your mind and heart with a pitchfork—or a steam shovel, if need be. You knew that already? You've already given it a real college try? The trouble is, something always seems to get in the way. That would be *you*.

How easily we play the blame game and point to others for our dilemma or lack of willpower. How easily we justify our out-of-control eating and unproductive spending.

❀ I work hard and I make very few demands for myself. Why on earth should I deny myself that Caramel

Macchiato on the way to work each morning? It's a small indulgence compared to jewelry or fine clothes or expensive trips. What difference does it make if I even finish the drink? I like wrapping my hand around that grande, extra large, super-duper, big-as-a-refrigerator to-go cup. I'm entitled to this splurge.

❊ I am far too stressed to think about nutrition. Healthy anything will have to wait until my life settles down. I want a bag of chips, and I want it *now*. This latest disappointment that just came my way is enough for me to deal with; I don't need the hassle of picking through wilted lettuce and limp radishes. I'm entitled to this treat.

Either of the two scenarios resonate with you? Me too. You *are* entitled to a little luxury in your day. And, as evidenced by a frantic fruitcake party of mine that you will soon read about, a dose of sugar and fat or a bit of spending sometimes gives you a psychological boost. (Don't even get me started on the merits of ice cream.)

But allow me to do a bit of deconstruction and turn that thinking inside out. What is the flip side of today's sense of entitlement?

You are also entitled to be able to sleep well at night because your bills are paid. You are entitled to the terrific feeling that comes from overcoming your entitlement urge *at least some of the time* as you proactively work toward debt control. You are entitled to a secure financial future. You are entitled

At $3 each day, not factoring the impulse muffin or the tip jar, that daily drink will set you back $15 each week or $780 a year. If you are in the habit of not finishing your drink, much of that $780 goes down the drain. Literally. Not too frugal.

to a sensible weight that does not overly tax your stamina, your bones, or your organs. You are entitled to the best health you can achieve, no matter your physical limitations, so you can fully enjoy your secure financial future.

> *Somewhere along the line sound stewardship has been replaced by a sense of entitlement.*
>
> JOSHUA YATES

Get Out Your Trusty Notebook!

Time for a quiz:

What is your honest-to-goodness goal for your life?

_____

What are your financial goals?

_____

What goals do you have for your body?

_____

What triggers your unproductive spending?

_____

What destructive spending habits do you have?

_____

What destructive eating habits do you have?

_____

What triggers bingeing or other unhealthy eating habits?

_____

What has sabotaged your budget before?

_____

What has sabotaged your diet before?

_____

Who (besides you) has sabotaged your budget?

_____

Who has had a positive impact on your financial life?

_____

Describe the most positive aspects of that person's...

      mind-set _____

      skill-set_____

      heart-set_____

What can you learn from that person?

_____

And Now to Reconstruct

When have you been successful at financial management?

_____

When have you been successful at weight loss and improved body health?

_____

What has been your strength?

_____

What circumstances surrounded your success?

_____

How can you recapture that time?

_____

Information

I stands for information. You are holding information in your hands right now. Information is what you already know and what you don't yet know.

Notebook! Write down what you know. Use an exercise like this to help you to isolate specifics:

Budget

I know that to successfully steward finances, I need to...

_____

To do that, I need to...

_____

In the past I have been successful when I've...

_____

My goals will work much better if these people help me along the way or hold me accountable:

_____

I can develop frugal skills by...

_____

I can develop restraint by reminding myself...

_____

I can live my life to the greater honor of God through...

_____

...and by reminding myself...

_____

Diet

I know that to successfully lose weight and to maintain a reasonably healthy body I need to...

_____

To do that, I need to...

_____

In the past I have been successful when I've...

_____

My goals will work much better if these people help me along the way or hold me accountable:

_____

I can develop healthy eating habits by...

_____

I can develop restraint by reminding myself...

_____

I can live my life to the honor of God through...

_____

...and by reminding myself...

_____

The weaknesses I discovered during deconstruction are...

_____

I need to acquire the following information and skill:

_____

If I am in over my head financially or suffering from eating disorders, I can find help at...

See? You already know a lot!

Look at any weaknesses you've uncovered so far. Will more information help you? Then educate yourself.

Information comes from everywhere: experience (*if* we learn the lessons it teaches us), other people's successes and failures, the history of previous generations, books, television programs, seminars, magazines, and thoughtful reflection upon and application of the Word of God. Try reading Proverbs!

> *We are almost entirely dependent on an economy of which we are almost entirely ignorant.*
>
> WENDELL BERRY

Try

T stands for try, try, and try again. This may be the crux of success or failure in weight or money issues (among others). Many of us are so practiced at failure we've resigned ourselves to—or become comfortable in—the loser's seat. (Based on what I've heard in my travels, I'm guessing that your "comfortable seat" is really more like a pincushion.)

Here's a news flash: Neither you nor I can ever stop trying. Paul knew this well when he wrote, "I do not understand what I do. For what I want to do I do not do, but what I hate I do" (Romans 7:15). Imagine if that sentiment stopped him from going forward with God's plan for *his* life!

We all bang into a couple of roadblocks when we try to work toward life's goals. Two of those roadblocks are life itself and our own mood.

The morning of January 10, 2004, was bitterly cold. Wonder Man and I awoke in our bedroom at our son's house. I padded into the bathroom to brush—and floss—my teeth. It was "new leaf" time, after all. I was ten days into the new year and the new me. (In spite of my good health and a somewhat satisfactory weight level, television appearances for my latest book gave me incentive to pare down a bit more.)

Are you as tired of trying as you are of failing?

I had a terrific morning planned: prayer, Pilates, dry brush my skin, a brisk two-mile walk, green tea and hearty steel-cut oats for breakfast, and water, water, water.

Toothbrush armed, I turned the faucet. Nothing. I tried the tub. Nothing. Straight to the kitchen I blasted. Another faucet—nothing. Since when did pipes freeze in Virginia?

With our son away and my husband sick with a bad cold, options were scarce. Within no time I was wrapped in a sleeping bag on the bare ground in the crawl space under the house, blow-dryer in hand. I spent a goodly amount of time down there, frozen into a squat position. I looked like a freeze-dried Russian mazurka dancer or one of those mummies dug up on the tundra and featured on the Discovery Channel.

As soon as I pried my frigid fingers off the blow-dryer and headed into the house, I was ready to eat a horse. You know what comes next, right? I thought nothing of ripping open a box that held *fruitcake* that had taken the brunt of jokes in our small family. Suddenly it was neither funny nor unappealing as I shoved a big chunk into my mouth, drooling from both corners.

When Life Gets in the Way of Living

When life gets in the way of living, you can't do a whole lot except sit on the cold ground and wait for pipes to thaw. The test of endurance and determination comes when you wake up the next day. Do you have another terrific morning planned? Or do you shrug off goals with "what's the use"? Here's another news flash: Regardless of your plan, your motivation, and your determination, *life will always get in the way*. Christians in particular distinguish themselves by how they handle themselves when troubles or interruptions come their way.

Experts claim that we should keep the equivalent of three months' pay in an accessible account for emergency use.

How does life get in our way? *Good grief!*

Cars need new transmissions. Heating bills go through the roof. Children make unexpected trips to the doctor. People lose jobs, fall ill, and sometimes die. Pipes freeze, property taxes skyrocket, Junior flushes your cell phone down the toilet. *Life happens.* And when it happens, it derails even the best plans.

In an ideal world, you would have an emergency fund to help you through rough times. Do I have an emergency fund? Yes. Did I always? No. Did I get derailed over and over? Yes.

I have also found that life derails my plan for healthy eating. Do I have a sensible approach to body image? Yes. Am I well informed about foods that benefit my body? Yes. Does life occasionally send me a curveball (or should I say *cheese* ball)? Yes. When my life becomes filled with the stress of busyness and deadlines or interrupts my plans, I eat like an idiot.

Psst...

Sometimes, I suspect, God is the one who gets in the way. Let me tell you about a young couple I recently met. Both are professional thirtysomethings. The woman stays home with three adopted children. Was it their lack of a financial plan? Was it the astronomical cost of adoption? Was it the addition of three robust little children? Who knows. This couple suddenly noticed the bottom line, and it was enough to scare the tar out of them. Savings and checkbook balances were literally diminishing before their terrified eyes.

Oh, how grand, no matter how hard, when "God happens" in my life!

"What should we do? We've got to get on top of things! And we want to adopt more children!"

Bingo. I had no doubt that God the Holy Spirit was giving this couple a nudge, a wake-up call. He'd already planted in their hearts a love and commitment for needy children—even if they didn't adopt another child. Now He was prompting them to "adopt" the financial skills to care for them.

As I listened to this remarkable woman share her story, I wondered if perhaps God has bigger plans in store for them, and they have to get their worldly affairs in working order first.

What a blessing! What a faithful God!

I'm Not in the Mood

Okay, fully human readers. If you can relate to either of the following, raise your hand.

Scenario number one: You're on your way home from Missy's tumbling class, all three kids in tow. The day has been a killer, and the last thing you want to do is become creative in the kitchen and make dinner—or even heat up leftovers. You just don't have the energy to deal with bellyaching from the under-ten crowd. You know a trip through the fast food restaurant will set you back about $20 (that you really don't have, not to mention you pledged not to spend unnecessary money this week), but you don't care. You're just not in the mood to cook.

Note from me: Where is it written that you'll stunt your kids' growth if you make them peanut butter and jam sandwiches for dinner? Real peanut butter, real jam, on healthy bread, served with whole milk, please, and a sliced apple.

Extra note from me: Kids prefer sandwiches sliced diagonally. I know these things.

Scenario number two: You're standing in front of the open fridge, door handle in hand, staring. You see many things, including crisp fruit, salad veggies, and homemade soup left over from dinner two nights ago. In addition to wasting electricity by standing there with that blank stare on your face, you pass on the good stuff and opt for a bag of chemical-laden microwave popcorn and several swipes at the Cool Whip and peanut butter with your right index finger. You're just not in the mood to eat veggies.

Note from me: Microwave popcorn and Cool Whip? Just for fun, put this book down and go read the ingredients. Go ahead. I'll wait. Check the peanut butter while you're at it. Be wary of the word "hydrogenated" or "natural flavors." Trust me.

What's behind this not-in-the-mood attitude?

I recently heard a popular speaker talk on the issue of order and clutter. I think she was trying to make points with the audience because she announced with the greatest aplomb that she'd never yet met a lazy person. I looked back at the television incredulously. *What? I've met plenty!* I would go so far as to put myself forward as a prime example. The flip side of my somewhat fabled nonstop drive is the fact that I'd sit around all day watching soaps and eating greasy potato chips if I could get away with it. But I can't. No one else can take care of my world the way I can. No one else can write this book. No one else understands my personal needs, the nuances of my body, what my body feels like, and how it reacts to different stimuli. And I am determined to serve, to honor God. And so I try. I try, try, and try again. I can never, ever give up trying. Neither can you.

Consumption

I am tempted to use C to promote contentment again. I'm opting instead for a word that I hope will stick with you like bathrobe lint, a word I hope will serve as a gentle reminder and a caution. I believe this word will aid you immeasurably with your weight and finances: *consumption*. This book talks a lot about consumption.

We are all consumers. Consumers consume. That means we buy and use goods and services. It also means we stick some things we buy into our mouths and chew and swallow. Nothing is wrong with that. But we get into trouble with the amount we consume.

We live in an environment that assures us not only that we deserve everything our heart desires but also that the way we are is not satisfactory and that happiness and satisfaction lie in consumption. So consume we do, as easy credit, unlimited selection, and unlimited availability has come to all but the least and most marginalized of us. Connect these dots, folks: We spend more and we eat more.

Do I consume to live or live to consume?

We have lost a sensible scale of economics and home life, and we're drowning in a world of plenty. Drowning in our body fat, drowning in our debt. Night after night we turn on the news and hear about our national economy, its economic indicators, the Dow Jones Average, and the like. All the while the numbers

fluctuate: up, down, up, down. Seesaw, seesaw. When I hear
the news reports, I think about countless people I've met for
whom no indicators will help until they are able to get a grip on
their profound indebtedness, fostered by this "gotta have it"
ethic. "The economy is picking up pace!" we hear from the
rosy-cheeked newscaster. How nice. Really. But tell *that* to
the average American family sitting on upward to $20,000 in
credit card debt. They would have a thing or two to say about
economic indicators. From all indications, their own personal
economics are in shambles.

> *Significantly the most striking feature of the
> ongoing furor over predatory marketing to college
> and high school students has been the
> adamant refusal of the credit card industry to
> acknowledge publicly its culpability.*
>
> ROBERT D. MANNING, *CREDIT CARD NATION*

And not only that, but for many of us, our uneasy,
unhealthy relationship with our own economics is just a small
part of the problem. We've also damaged our relationships
with our environment, our community, our heretofore sacred
family ties, and our skill-sets. We rarely feel deeply satisfied,
but the problem is not that we don't have everything we want.
Rather, we feel lost and alone because of these damaged relationships. With this book in hand, you can begin restoring
those relationships by developing your own new and improved
Christian "home economics" for the twenty-first century.

I do not intend to become overly nostalgic, but has anyone
else noticed that we have way more stuff to care for than our
grandparents did? And way more activity. And way more
paperwork. And storage units. And clutter-reduction seminars.

And bins. And scales. And diet drinks. Stuff. Obscene amounts of stuff to worry about and hoard while we "stuff" our bodies with obscene servings of food.

Been to a restaurant lately? My mom used to serve her three daughters and herself with what shows up as one meal these days! Yes, I know we can eat half of what's served in a restaurant and bring the rest home for later. My point is that we ourselves are turning into grande, extra-large, super-duper, refrigerator-sized people.

The amount we consume is one of the single most important factors in maintaining physical and financial health. I tackle this issue head-on in my chapter called "The 50 Percent Principle."

Wonder Man and I have traveled extensively in the past few years, leaving home for months on end. Besides the comfort of our own bed, we leave behind lots of stuff. All the stuff we think we need, the stuff we feel we can't live without. Guess what happens from the second we close the door behind us? All that stuff doesn't matter, and we find we can live without it rather well. As a bonus, our stress level plummets.

Health

H stands for health. A healthy weight. A healthy checkbook balance.

Many women are taking a hard look at where popular culture has been shoving them, and they are starting to shove back. But some are shoving in a frustrated, undirected way. They have a lot less concern for keeping up with the latest fashion or home-tending magazine and less concern with image and calories, but they are frustrated all the same. Frustrated with failure, wanting something they can grab hold of and run with, but not another gimmick or quick fix. Wanting health in everything. Balance. Moderation. Reasonableness. Looking for someone to toss a life preserver their way. *Something.* Are you one of those women?

Suppose someone said to you: "Every time I hit my finger with a hammer, it hurts." What would you say?

"Well...don't hit yourself with the hammer!"

Suppose every time you ate sugar you spiked your blood sugar, craved even more sugar, ate more, and became fatter and fatter? *Well...don't eat sugar.* Or learn about the glycemic index so you eat sugars intelligently. (In my opinion, diabetes is going to become a national crisis before long—and what on earth are we doing to our children!)

Suppose every time you went into one of those big-box discount stores (without specific need or purpose) you ended up finding something irresistible—even though you were perfectly content with life before you walked through the automatic doors. *Well...don't go into those stores.* Or don't shop unless you have a specific need. What's up with this shopping-for-fun routine we've developed, anyway? If you want fun, go to a park.

Get a Grip

Throughout this book I've been hinting at something: *Get a grip.*

Yeah, well, that's the problem, Wonder Woman! you scream, flinging said book across the living room floor. Again, I totally agree. That *is* the problem.

Physical Health

How do you get a grip on bodily health? You begin with a complete physical. I am holistic about my physical well-being, partly because of my sisters, Sheila and Anne, who have positively influenced me with regard to alternative medicine or exercise. I regularly see two chiropractic physicians, Rick Kahler and Chad Hawk, and I rely on my friend and medical doc, Pam Oerhtman, for general care and upkeep. I mention these people by name in appreciation for their genuine concern for me.

Financial Health

How do you get a grip on financial health? Exactly the same way. You start with a complete physical:

❋ Open your mail and say agh!

❋ *Notebook!* Chart all of your vital statistics: your fixed, discretionary, and long-term expenses as well as your income.

❋ Give yourself a thorough internal checkup: Track your money for a few weeks to see where you spend it. Write down every expenditure just as you would keep track of the food you eat by writing down every morsel.

❋ Have a bedside chat with your mate or others who participate in the financial income or outgo in the family. This includes age-specific chats with children.

❋ Don't forget psychiatric evaluation! (Just kidding.) But you do have to look at the mental "health" of your spending habits.

❋ Acquire a few good books or workbooks to help you plan a healthy regimen. (I heartily recommend my book *Living Well on One Income* [Harvest House Publishers], for 232 pages of practical tips, strategies, protocols, and fun.)

This Has Got to Matter

Your physical and financial health absolutely *must* matter to you! Remember my allusion to my age? Fifty-seven by the time this book is released. And though I am financially solvent now, I can look back at years upon years of hardship that I could have avoided. Financial health was possible along the way; I know that now. And oh, the stress I could have prevented! What lasting effect has that stress had on my body? How could I have benefited others through better stewardship of my money in the past? And let's not even *talk* about the arguments with Joe that could have been avoided.

I can also point to my feet that ache from a lifetime of improperly fitted shoes, and cellulite that makes my thighs look like a wall painting of an Etruscan ruin. I can point to overly plucked eyebrows, muscles that have turned to lard, and teeth that need a major overhaul. I was always too busy, too overwhelmed, too broke to be proactive with my health and appearance.

Women's bodies are not what they were meant to be due to a lack of real food. They are literally starving. Skipping meals increases the likelihood of getting fatter because the metabolism slows down due to lack of something to digest.

MY SISTER SHEILA

Whew!

Be content. Honor God. Deconstruct. Inform yourself. Try, try again. Watch your consumption. Think of your health. *Do these directions ever end? All of this work sounds daunting.*

Oh, stop. Once you find a better way to live, improving your situation is not hard at all. It becomes second nature. You are taking the first steps as you use this book to

❀ ask yourself why you eat and spend the way you do

❀ assess the risk you take when you do not consider a change of perspective

❀ set a course for greater peace and contentment in your life

You can look forward to having money in the bank (for those emergencies) and to feeling good about your body image (even if there are hanger marks in the last dress you wore).

Forest ranger, cowgirl, veterinarian, journalist—flights of fancy aside, had I gone to college for anything, I'm sure I would have become a teacher. Teaching is built into who I am. Everything that comes out of my mouth is information, instruction, advice. (Ask my poor family.)

Yet to teach, one first has to learn. Other people have influenced me besides those I've mentioned. I have followed their steps on my path to better living. We will meet them in the next chapter.

The Tale of a Bad Day

Still smarting from what you consider a lackluster presentation this morning, you start your search for the car keys. Abandoning your purse, you check your coat pockets, and your hand goes clear through to the lining. Five minutes into your search you find the keys on the bottom of a plastic bag in which you brought a baby-shower gift.

No time for lunch. You grab the granola bar you just found in your desk and run out the door. Before you get Junior from preschool and deposit him at childcare to join his little sister, you hit the ATM for the third time this week. It's not with your bank but the drive-up is convenient when you don't have much time.

Junior decides this is the day to examine every piece of gravel poking through the snow in the preschool parking lot, but you soon have him in his car seat, which is several layers thick with pretzels, animal cracker pieces, and cheddar cheese goldfish. As you buckle him in, you notice his socks don't match.

Right on cue, Precious throws a fit when you drop off Junior, and she smears residual SpaghettiOs over your wool pants. Junior joins the chorus: *Waaagghh!* Guilt again. You bribe Junior with a promise to buy a new Disney video before you rush back to the car, leaving Precious in a wail. Animal cracker pieces never looked so good.

On the way back to the office you stop to pick up dry cleaning, but the cleaners appear to be out to lunch too. A cardboard clock on the door says "Back at one." You fume as you head back to your car, which you parked illegally a block away. How on earth did a parking control officer leave that ticket on your windshield in so short a time? Impossible! You shove the ticket into your purse, a nagging reminder of the ticket you got last month. Let's see: disorganized home manager, mediocre employee, candidate for Bad Mommy of the Year, and now scofflaw. Yep, sounds like a typical day...

Back at work, you're greeted with two messages on your voice mail: one from Hubby-Dearest, one from Missy. Something about Thai food tonight and going to a friend's house after school. Right now the idea of Thai take-out is very appealing, and if Missy goes to her friend's, she'll probably stay for dinner, so (God forgive you) that is one less child to deal with after work. The day is looking up...

To be continued...

4
The Relational Reconnect

⟐

An administrator at a long-term care facility once told me that when one of their residents died it was as if a library filled with rare, old books had burned.

SUSAN CORT JOHNSON

Life is a continual "before" and "now." Each day is a domino, tipping over and tapping the next dawn, which itself falls away to the next day, leaving a place we call a memory, a place we call "before." Things will always have been different "before," and things will always be different now. Each domino will tip until all of life becomes a nostalgic blur.

What if we push the dominoes back in the other direction? What if we stand them up and give a gentle poke to send them tipping backward? What if together we stop the loss of "before" and push our way into yesterday?

I wondered about this out loud one day as my mother and I wandered back in reverie to a "before" kind of place—before, when I was young; before, when women like Josie Pietrowski were backdoor neighbors and friends (or as my Polish grandmother would say of Josie: pests); before, when things were different.

"I'll tell you what if," said my mother. "Your grandmother would turn over in her grave!"

Who Was Josie and Why Does It Matter?

Josie Pietrowski was one of the women I grew up with. I place her in the same category as other friends of my grandmother, women like Pani Galka and Pani Raczkowska. They were a private club, a sisterhood who waved the Polish flag and danced the polka. They were friends who spoke to each other in lusty syllables and wore cotton dresses with heavy stockings rolled down around their ankles. They had chin whiskers and permed white hair, and they played bingo every Tuesday night. They were voices that brought meaning to my existence whether I understood their language or not. Josie worked her way into the club not only because of her nationality but also because of geography: Her house was at the end of a forbidding path along the wood behind our house, a path that bode ill even to this intrepid pioneer of tree tops and secret paths of my own. The path to Josie's house scared me.

Though the path was probably no more than 100 feet long before it opened into a clearing between Josie's garage and flower garden, I ran the length of it holding my breath and wishing I could have run with my eyes closed. The fact that Josie emerged from that path with irritating regularity, which is why my grandmother would be in a snit right now, gave her an extraordinary presence and power. I thought she just might be a little special because of it. My Polish grandmother, "Babci," just thought she was a pain in the neck.

Josie was a backdoor neighbor before things changed. She was a woman who held court with other women. I doubt she sought counsel or gave counsel as much as she delighted in gossip. She was the yenta in the group. Every group had, needed, and probably deserved a yenta. Josie may have thought her manifest destiny was to gossip. For her, this was a rather enjoyable way to spend an afternoon as women with babushkas on their heads sat and blabbed.

Josie's forays were not limited to backyard neighbors. On the bus she would go downtown to the large Polish community, marching boldly, her narrow shoulders pressing ahead while her large behind tagged along. Watch out! Here comes Josie! Women wiped heavy hands on aprons and set out cold prune pierogi, rye bread, and coffee heavy with milk as Josie told them the latest—I am sure—of what went on at our house. Back and forth she went, her poor command of English punctuated by rolling *r*s and hard *t*s, always appearing at our house in time for dinner.

Babci would curse in Polish when she saw Josie coming. She would fly into a rage when Josie poked her nose into the stew pot. And then Babci would set another place at the table. Her curiosity got the better of her every time as the two of them wrapped themselves in the comfort of familiar sounds and drank cappuccino long before it was vogue, Josie's trademark toothpick protruding from her mouth. I wish I had a Josie in my life.

"I see what you mean," said my mother. "Things are different now."

> *It is the mothers, not the warriors, who create a people and guide their identity.*
>
> STANDING BULL

What Do I Mean?

Our backyards don't connect any more. Josie is gone. So is Pani Galka. And Pani Raczkowska. And Babci. That's what I mean. Many of us have lost female bonding and backdoor neighbors, and we run breathlessly down scary paths with no safe clearing in sight.

Women need to connect. All women share a vital bond and interact in a universal sorority through experience, but for many of us, intimate connections are fraying like the cord on an old toaster. We are becoming disconnected and unplugged, and we have little left but the constant tip of dominoes. We are falling away from each other faster than ever before. We are estranged from our past generations and from our present sisterhood, and this estrangement is costing us plenty.

As a young child, I enjoyed a sense of belonging, a sense of community, and a sense of security. I felt safe as I pushed my little body back into the big maw of Pani Galka's flower-print couch, tapping the sides of my shiny patent leather shoes together and listening to the sounds of rolling *rs*. I, the acolyte, the shadow, the domino waiting my turn to have, to know, to even *be* a Josie.

But life caught me on the swell of a giant wave and washed me away to private places of my own choice, away from the backyard wood, away from any chance of community, and into myself. Though I'm quite happy to feel self-confident, my spirit mourns the loss of others. Others of the sisterhood, others who can poke their noses into my stew pot, hormone for hormone. Others who might raise their voices and speak to me about what's happening downtown. Others, like Josie, who aren't in our lives anymore. Others who left and took their skills (and stew-pot recipes) with them.

> *For when community falls, so must fall all the things that only*
> *community life can engender and protect: the care of the old,*
> *the care and education of children, family life, neighborly*
> *work, the handing down of memory, the care of the earth,*
> *respect for nature and the lives of wild creatures.*
>
> WENDELL BERRY

Everybody *Does* Love Raymond!

Know why movies like *My Big Fat Greek Wedding* and television shows like *Everybody Loves Raymond* are so successful? They resonate with us, that's why. As broken and dysfunctional as those families seem, we envy them because a faint memory deep inside us yearns for the connectedness we get from the whole lot—from grandparents, siblings, cousins, aunts and uncles, and even pesty next-door neighbors.

The Generational Disconnect

Times change. Society changes. We have lost a precious and necessary connection to our past. The phone line has been disconnected before any conversation could even transpire, and the phone has been ripped right out of our hands. Sometimes "wireless" just means "detached."

Distance, technology, and cultural norms have ripped us away from our root systems and support systems. This is both worrisome and tragic. The Puritan ethic of thrift was once embedded in our social consciousness, providing strong and virtuous financial and physical boundaries. But now we are encountering the "erosion of the traditional cognitive connect," according to Robert D. Manning, in his book *Credit Card Nation* (Basic Books, 2000), which reads better than a Stephen King thriller. (A must read for anyone who wants to understand America's escalating dependence on credit.)

The first thing to go when you are busy is friendship.

We bemoan the loss of that awareness and connection to time-honored skills and values, but we scream loud and clear that we do not want to retrofit our personal or social reality to conform to an illusory past. We don't want to sport Josie's toothpick or big behind, but we do want her strength of community, her skills, her recipes...and we want them modified to cut the fat. Deep inside, we cannot help but long for the simple and connected life that Josie and her friends shared. Even from our advanced perspective, some aspects to that life just seemed better.

Generational separation occurs for many reasons. But we learn to develop relationships and grow in virtue as we integrate generations in small families and in larger social structures. This integration doesn't just happen. We must be purposeful and realistic as we construct our immediate families, extended families, and communities.

Make no mistake—generational integration is more than putting the "grand" back in grandparenting or tearing down backyard barriers. It addresses our separation from that which has gone before us. It questions our fiercely independent, self-determining, and lonely struggle to survive the pressures of twenty-first-century life. We've cast off the old in favor of the new, but the new is too illusive, too mercurial. We're weary of keeping up, of chasing an impossible dream. We are no longer standing at an unmistakable trailhead with paths clearly marked and blazed. I am not convinced we can find our way or our identity on our own. We need a generational reconnect.

Connecting with Our Own Generation Is Important Too

In addition to learning from those who have walked the trail before us, women, in particular, need someone to walk with *now*. Life as a lonely hiker is downright hard. Women are mourning the loss of each other and yearning to replace their independent, isolated existence with camaraderie (and all of its attendant quirks). Women need to talk and laugh and cry with other women. Unfulfilled, that need creates restlessness and robs our peace. I know what I'm talking about. I have felt that

restlessness many times through the years as my indepen-
dence and busyness have put a strain on vital relationships.

Researchers suspect that women have a different
behavioral response to stress than men. When a hormone called oxytocin is released in a woman, she
feels compelled to protect her children and gather
with other women. This has calming effects. Several
studies have found that social ties reduce women's
risk of disease by lowering blood pressure, heart
rate, and cholesterol. One study found that people
who had no friends increased their risk of prema-
ture death. In another study, those who had the
most friends cut their risk of death over a nine-year
period by more than 60 percent. Harvard's famous
Nurses' Health Study found that the more friends
women had, the less likely they were to develop
physical impairments as they aged, and the more
likely they were to be leading a joyful life. Purdue
University conducted a study that concluded that
girls want someone to share secrets with. (Boys want
a pal with whom to share activities.)

No Time!

While going to extremes with "The Tale of a Bad Day," I'm
not far off base. That composite woman is one busy lady! As
are we all. We pack each day full of chores, work, agendas, husbands, children, and activities. Our bodies are exhausted, but
still we strain to keep everything from toppling on our heads.
Try as we may, we cannot cram one more thing into our schedules. It is here that relationships suffer. Any kind of relationship—even a phone connection—requires a time commitment.
Yet we've run out of time. It is hard to balance career and
family—or *just* career or *just* family for that matter.

We are booked solid. Our daily planners are stuffed with dry cleaning stubs, phone messages, and gas receipts. Our busyness causes a deadly consequence: isolation. Where did this busyness come from?

I don't want to sound like some recluse who lives in a cave and trims her wicks, but I believe busyness has come from the very technology that was designed and promoted to make our lives simpler. It has enslaved and detached us. We are running ourselves ragged, and we are isolated from any real sense of community. Technology has obscured or obliterated our inter-connectedness. Let's talk about "before" and "now" for illustration:

❀ Once upon a time, we went for walks and nodded hello to others along our way. Now we are shut off from the world as we zoom from chore to chore in climate-controlled cars—with windows closed, no less.

❀ Once upon a time, we sat outside, where *front* porches became news hubs for the neighborhood. (Let me say that again: *front*.) Now we are shut off from the world, holed up inside climate-controlled houses and occupied with television or computers as board games languish on closet shelves and kitchen tables collect clutter instead of the clash of ideas or the good will of friends.

❀ Once upon a time, kids walked to school, rode their bikes, or rode the big yellow bus. Now we drive them to and from school. We feel we have to, not simply because they are busy with before- *and* after-school programs but because we are worried for their safety.

❀ Once upon a time we wrote letters or heard about friends far and near through the neighborhood grapevine coffee klatch. Now we have e-mail, faxes, pagers, and cell phones. Long distance companies compete for our business.

❀ Once we lingered after dinner while one of us washed and the other dried. Now we pile plates and pans in our dishwashers and race to answer the buzzer on the clothes dryer.

❀ Once we played rummy at night or watched a little television. Now we have 24-hour programming, DVDs, virtual sound, real sound, and must-see television.

We don't have time for friendship, and we barely have time for family members. Let's flip this one inside out too, shall we?

When we don't make the time for relationships, aren't we putting material gain and *things* ahead of people? Isn't that pretty stupid?

1. When a family's house burns, what is the first thing they say? "At least we escaped with our *things!*" Nope. "At least we have *each other!*" At times of loss or tragedy, we are shaken and vulnerable, and we need each other. We instantly become relational. So why should we wait for tragedy?

2. Let's look at our justification for all of our striving and hard work:

   ✩ We have to pay the rent or mortgage on this luxury house. (That payment is for a thing.)
   Note from me: So move to a more affordable place and reduce your next mortgage.

   ✩ Our kids have to go to that school so they can have a better future. (That is, so they can get a good job, make money, and buy more things.)
   Note from me: How much are they learning about relationship, community, or family ties?

About family hikes in the wonders of fall foliage, about lazing around with hot cocoa in front of a fireplace? Listen well: You better make time while you have it. Far too many people run out of time and look back at a life that wasn't lived at all.

The Coworker Connection

Of course, not all changes are bad. They're just changes. Once, women were in the home (for the most part). Then they ran to the office. Now they *run* the office! Yet women will always be relational and communal, regardless of where they are. So can't other women in the workplace satisfy their intrinsic need for community? Hey! Kill two birds with one stone: Deal with the time issue *and* find community...

Can relationships at the workplace replace what is missing? I asked a group of friends, and their answers are revealing:

Ashby: "Workplace takes on a different role. It's all about production."

Helen: "There's a fine line between 'personal' and 'business.' "

Shirley: "Women today have too much on their minds. They can't find time for really close friends, no matter where they are."

Ann: "A woman doesn't have time to build many relationships, especially beyond the workplace. When she gets home, she has to make up for what she didn't have time to do during the day."

Iris: "Yeah, but when you take away work, nothing is left. At work you share day-to-day."

Rae: "I can see that women try to fill that void at work, but the whole relationship is different."

Shirley: "Not to mention that there is very often a gap in ages."

Rae: "I think that's good. I mean, if you had a backdoor neighbor, who's to say she couldn't be older?"

Ann: "Or younger."

Ashby: "Yeah, just like having aunts and your grandma."

Iris: "This is all about relationships. Bottom line, it's hard to have one with everything else going on. It's not like all you do is sit around the house and eat bonbons and drink coffee with neighbors. Those days are over."

Shirley: "I wish they weren't. I'd like to eat bonbons with a friend."

What to Do, What to Do

So how do we integrate within our own generation *and* intergenerationally (older and younger), both at home and within society, in order to appropriate skills and resourcefulness to help navigate our path to a better life?

Needless to say, I have some suggestions. Why not read them out loud to your family tonight and get a good, old-fashioned conversation going?

I'll Dry!

We used to dry our dishes. We built community and spanned a multitude of generations when we dawdled over dishes. Dinner table talk of one's day turned to more earnest and private discussion over those sodden dish towels, and children learned to share duties and rewards. Children also learned the importance of an ordered environment: We cook dinner, we eat dinner, and we wash the dishes. A whole lot of skills came along with drying dishes. Now we feel happy if our children bring their dirty plates to the dishwasher. No, wait—*now* we don't even know how to *load* the dishwasher correctly!

Sit long, talk much. And eat bonbons.

Should we bring back the dish towel—for its original use, that is? The choice, of course, is yours. Once you consider the cost of energy to run your dishwasher every day, you may opt for this. Getting into the practice of hand washing and towel drying dishes is a monumental effort, however, and I do not recommend *anything* that will set you up for failure—you've probably had enough of that.

Look at your life. If you live with others, what can you do within your household routine to promote connectedness? Can you congregate as a family to eat dinner every night (or at least most nights) *no matter what*? Can you say a quick prayer together in the morning to start the day? Can you reserve an inviolable half-hour to share with your children every night before bed?

When are all of you often in one place at the same time each day? Do something meaningful with that time.

Cars and Trains and Planes

"Distance" used to be how far down the lane it was to the mailbox, or how long it took to walk to school, or the half-hour it took to drive to Gram's and Gramp's for Sunday dinner. (An eternity!) Today, "distance" is far greater than the other side of town or a short way into the country, and the change has wrought terrible damage.

Some distance and separation is necessary. Without a doubt, the realities of continuing education, marriage, armed services, job requirements, and plain old spread-your-wings adventure are good reasons for distance between family members. Virtual cold wars have also created distance between family members.

But enforced separation has gone beyond the pale. We have slipped into the notion that an empty nest *mandates* separation, and we no longer think of ourselves as a part of a greater whole. This is problematic, though many grandparents are moving closer to adult children and grandchildren, creating a stable generational connection.

Bring Back the Sunday Dinner!

This is my passion. If you can't do dishes, if you can't gather for prayer, if you can't do anything else, do this: Bring back the Sunday dinner and make your fellowship a holy offering to the Lord. Set your table with the abundance of God's blessing, throw open your doors to others, and feast on the fantastic joy of the Lord's Day. Fill your house with music, with chatter, and with thanks. The practice of Sunday dinner is an incredible legacy to give your children.

How I cherished our Sunday ritual, when all of my extended family would gather at someone's house after church. I remember Aunt Clara's big white bowl with black polka dots, Aunt Lil's Pyrex casserole filled with the *best* Jell-O concoctions, Uncle Bill's goofy chuckle, and Uncle Walter's trickster spirit. I remember mashed potatoes and meatloaf and peas and noise and yelling and laughter. I remember running and playing with cousins and friends until it was too dark to see. I remember the very *smell* of my cousin Rit's pigeon coop, my cousin Johnny's drop-dead good looks, and my cousin Tom's temper tantrums. I remember scuffed shoes, scraped knees, and dirty hands. And it all centered on the ritual of the Sunday dinner.

We all need ritual. Children, in particular, benefit from family rituals. What better pillar and symbol of community than Sunday dinner (regardless of how small your family)? I call that a better way to live!

> *Dear Auntie Dumpling* [that would be me] *& Uncy Joe:*
> *We wanted to tell you how awesome it was to have you*
> *near us when we were growing up. We learned a lot*
> *from you. Our special birthdays were a blast. And it*
> *meant a lot that we could call you*
> *when we needed to talk. We love you!*
>
> LIV & LEAH (NIECES)

Connected Kids

How grateful I am that our grandchildren have parents who recognize the importance of free play with other children. Learning how to negotiate social constraints, taboos, and expectations within peer groups is part of a child's development. Unfortunately, adults structure too much of a child's playtime these days. I am not for a *heartbeat* suggesting that we let the little munchkin run rampant or unprotected, but I do feel that we need to let our children learn to work with their peers. This is not necessarily accomplished in school.

> Children are
> old before they
> are young.
>
> FRANK PERETTI

It is incumbent upon us as parents, grandparents, guardians, and advocates of children to ensure a safe, secure, and carefree home life. We should hook them to our suspenders and teach them how to negotiate the twists and turns in the path ahead of them. We are the ones to show them how to overcome barriers, walk on slippery trails, and avoid dangerous pitfalls. We should also let them see how we climb out of the pits we fall into. Modeling behavior for our children is utterly critical, especially habits that relate to body image or finances.

❋ What kind of message are we sending our children when they see Mom or Dad constantly whipping out a piece of plastic to pay for things? Or when they overhear arguments about money? What kind of message are we sending our children when we ourselves are manipulated by the siren call of crafty ad campaigns and act like it's cute to "shop till we drop"?

❋ What kind of message are we sending our children (particularly our little girls) when we become slaves to body image?

Note from me: I do not like Barbie. So guess what? Someone gave our granddaughter a Barbie doll. I am constantly hiding that thing behind furniture, under heavy appliances, or waaay back in dresser drawers. I even hid it behind the ice cream in the freezer... hmm...I see the error of my ways there. How that thing keeps surfacing is beyond me.

According to one study, in 2002 children aged 4–12 spent $30 billion of their own money (a third of it on sweets, somewhat less on toys). In 2001 children 12–19 spent $172 billion of their own money.

Children are increasingly involved in our consumer culture, and marketers specifically target ads for toys and food toward kids. Marketers set many of the social, cultural, and normative concepts of childhood. Dominating companies such as Disney wield incredible social power. Younger and younger children are making purchasing decisions, and marketers scrutinize *everything* kids do. Fool them. Send your kids into the backyard armed with a jump rope, a tennis ball, and a friend. The sales sharks will never find them there.

What is missing is...the secret weapon: moms know.
They know because they stand in the stream of mother
knowledge that rolls back for millennia. They know
because they stand in a community of
experienced mothers of all ages.

FREDERICA MATHEWES-GREEN

Be a Friend

What if you live alone and have no immediate or extended family? If you live within a city, develop a walking routine and meet others along the way. If safety is an issue, find an environment that you can visit regularly: a library, a coffee house, or a club. Many churches sponsor singles' groups. A friend of mine once said, "It takes a friend to be a friend." If you are all alone and needing a friend, be one first. (Just be cautious: predators are out there.)

No Greater Friend

In chapter 1, I talked about Jesus Christ transforming my life. In chapter 2, I boldly proclaimed that our motivation to steward anything should be our love for God and our identity in Christ.

It seems logical that a word on *spiritual* connectedness should complete my thoughts in this chapter.

Suppose I stood in front of a room of strangers and asked for a show of hands from those who have felt disconnected from God or from the body of Christ at one time in their lives. I sincerely believe every hand would shoot up.

Is there a soul alive who hasn't felt hurt or embarrassed by the church, confused by different Christian doctrines, battered by the world, or abandoned by God?

I have felt all of those emotions and more, and I'm not going to lie to you: A spiritual reconnect can be hard.

Hooking my soul to the cross of Christ after decades of jargon and bluster has at times left me shaken and frail. It's been horrifically hard, frankly, to plumb deeply, down into hidden-away heart muscle never before flexed, to find that most primal and excuseless love of God. At times, all I could muster was a pretty solid Christian vocabulary that sat on the surface and animated all my outward appearances just enough to make me presentable (acceptable) to watching eyes. It took the Word of God—the really and truly appropriated Word of

God—to pierce my heart, to penetrate, to lance, and to wound my soul.

Renew a right spirit within me, was my plea. *Renew a right spirit within me.*

In the next chapter we will take a brief look at the fruit of that Spirit, the Holy Spirit of God, who I hope and pray is renewing your heart and your soul this very day.

The Tale of a Bad Day

Work goes well in the afternoon. A little tweaking here and there, some productive conversation in the break room, and you click on "Send" with a sense of accomplishment. Your interoffice e-mail will redeem your presentation that morning.

The neighbor calls. Barky broke through the fence and is raiding the garbage—and how come Missy didn't come home as she does every day after school? You can't bring yourself to ask that sweet old lady to round up your dog again. It's much too cold and icy. A call to Hubby-Dearest ends in a hushed, furious impasse. He can't leave work and you can't leave work. Barky is on her own. Maybe the snow that's predicted will cover the mess she makes.

You find comfort in sharing this episode with coworkers. This is a good group; you feel valued and understood here. Sympathy flows when one of you has a problem—to a point. You've learned that very specific lines cannot be crossed at work. Others will cover for you and carry you and listen to you—to a point.

You're in a pretty good mood when you leave work, and sing with the kids when you pick them up. Precious shows signs of nodding off, however, as the car heater incubates her in her warm clothes. You turn up the volume on her favorite cassette. Don't sleep now! You'll never get to bed tonight!

You drive by the arches on the way back to the cleaners—a fatal mistake. Junior does not miss a trick. His wail, anyway, should keep Precious awake. You succumb to his demands and swing through the drive-through. After all, the kids don't like Thai. This precludes rustling up dinner for them. Precious gets in on the excitement: She knows, she knows. Yippee Meals and french fries are coming!

To the cleaners. Not a parking space is in sight, so you leave the car in that same illegal parking space. (Does the first ticket count for two stops, sort of like a two-for-one special?) You have to schlep both kids and their fries through cold slush to get the cleaning. Like an idiot, you spent your cash at the fast food joint and leave the cleaners empty-handed.

Buckling in Precious and Junior, your eye catches sight of the seriously overdue DVDs. But the snow and traffic is getting too much for you. So home you go, only to be greeted by Barky, stubby little tail wagging and dirty disposable diapers everywhere.

To be continued...

5
Fruitful Living

*But the fruit of the Spirit is love, joy, peace,
patience, kindness, goodness, faithfulness,
gentleness, and self-control.*

THE APOSTLE PAUL

Together we've asked our hearts the question why. We've honestly examined our motives and considered a strategy to help us to live a better life through the DITCH method.

We've taken a look at our critical need for the wisdom and support of others. We've dusted off furniture, evaluated resolutions, and considered the effect of sin. We've recognized our call to honor and thank God, considered a holistic approach to weight and finances, and finally understood why everyone does love Raymond.

Throughout, I've made a deliberate attempt to provoke thought and to get you to connect the dots. By asking questions, by turning issues inside out, by considering deepest cause, reason, or effect, I hoped to evoke an "Oh, I get it!" moment or two as you turned the pages.

As we head toward part 2, which is the practical approach (skill-set) to DITCHing the diet and the budget, it is only right to wind down part 1 by considering the role of God the Holy Spirit in all of this.

You want to get a grip on your weight and finances, and you want to live a better life. I assume you are a Christian or are open to Christian sensibilities. I am a Christian too. I can't write a book on living a better life without bringing God into it. Talk about putting the cart before the horse!

Just as my sister Sheila awoke me one morning with exciting possibilities for my life, I believe God can awaken us to new hope through the fruit of the Spirit, which naturally grows in the life of a person who is indwelt by the Spirit of God. Once fruit is in our lives, the quality of our lives in Christ will be enhanced, and we will influence those around us. I call that a better life.

The Wish Rock

Many years ago, our family began a charming ritual of finding a rock circled by a white stripe, bringing the rock to the edge of a body of water, closing our eyes, and flinging it over our shoulders into the water. Onlookers watched the ripples fade and disappear and then told us when it was "safe" to open our closed eyes. As the Yates' legend goes, if you follow this formula, your wish will come true.

What can I do, through God's grace, to make my wishes come true?

Sometimes I wander alone along shores of lakes or rivers to think and pray. Every now and then my eye catches hold of a white-striped stone. I bend down and grab the irresistible rock and go to water's edge. I close my eyes tight and fling, and I wait for wishes to come true. Do you ever wish?

Wishes are as varied as rocks themselves. Some are big and bold, some small and simple. Some wishes are whimsical, and some have eyebrow-crunching sincerity. Some wishes are too private or painful to share. Such is the way with wish rocks.

And such is the way with my wishes when I commune with the Holy One and fling white-banded rocks over my shoulder.

What Do You Wish For?

Do you ever wish, as I do, that you could be more like Jesus? That you could somehow break the bonds of destructive behavior and let your light shine like a field light at a football game? Do you wish that you could be free from the bondage of weight and money issues? Do you wish that your relationships were healthier, that you could show more kindness, that peace would come to your tortured soul?

Or has your experience convinced you to wish only for whimsy and to never trust your heart to wishes made of stone? Is the fruit of your life anger, melancholy, turmoil, impatience, selfishness, gossip, bitterness, harshness, and a lack of control? (The flip side is love, joy, peace, patience, kindness, goodness, faithfulness, gentleness, and self-control.)

This book is my eyebrow-crunching wish that you will put your trust in the truest Rock of all, the Rock on whom your weary soul can rest, the Rock whose promises for you will all come true. My wish is that you will find a better life. But it all begins with you. You've got to bend a little to clutch His promise in your hand, to feel the certainty of His grace, and to release yourself in complete surrender to His Spirit.

Notebook! Make a wish:

My wish for my financial security is

_____.

My wish for my body is

_____.

My wish for my spiritual walk is

_____.

My wish for my family is

_____.

Get Out of the Way

Jesus said we must pick up our cross daily and follow Him. Here is a simple paraphrase: Die to self. (When you picked up your cross in Christ's neighborhood, you weren't going to a picnic.)

Have you ever wondered why Christians talk so much of dying to self? It is because it gets us out of the way, and then the Holy Spirit can have His way with us.

It is popular to think you are captain of your own ship. Yet if most of us are honest, we will admit our navigational skills usually end up with rudders hopelessly stuck in the mud of our latest fiasco. The Lord our God invites us to let Him take the helm. He knows the way through still water and through white water to safe sailing. He even has experience with storms.

Jesus said in John 14, "If you love me, you will obey what I command. And I will ask the Father, and he will give you another Counselor to be with you forever—the Spirit of truth. The world cannot accept him, because it neither sees him nor knows him. But you know him, for he lives with you and will be in you." *If* you get out of the way! Let God the Holy Spirit have His way with you. Hand over that tiller!

But what happens when we live God's way?
He brings gifts into our lives, much the same way that
fruit appears in an orchard—things like affection for
others, exuberance about life, serenity. We develop will-
ingness to stick with things, a sense of compassion in the
heart, and a conviction that a basic holiness permeates
things and people. We find ourselves involved in loyal
commitments, not needing to force our way in life, to
marshal and direct our energies.

EUGENE PETERSEN, *THE MESSAGE*

Notebook!

Am I afraid to "let go and let God"?

_____.

Is my fear based on lack of trust, shame, or pride?

_____.

How can I begin to let God the Holy Spirit have His way with me...

at home _____

at work _____

at church _____

at play _____

Galatians 5

In Galatians 5:22-23, Paul lists the indwelling virtues of Christian life that we have mentioned: love, joy, peace, patience, kindness, goodness, faithfulness, gentleness, and self-control. They are not optional or arbitrary. *Each and every one of these grows in us if we live by the Spirit of God.*

Have we been indifferent to these virtues? Have we wrapped them in fine linen and put them in a drawer to use on special occasions? Or do we share the beauty of these virtues by using them daily like sturdy utensils or dazzling china? Do we set them before our guests, a show of Christian hospitality that is filled to the rim with tasty delight? Does our cup run over? Paul said it well: "Since we live by the Spirit, let us keep in step with the Spirit" (Galatians 5:25). May I paraphrase? "Hey, you Galatians! Put your denarius where your mouth is! Let's see a little action!"

It is time to look at the fruit of the Spirit in a fresh way, to unlock the chambers in our hearts and shake a little dust off our souls. Let's invite the clean, strong wind of the Holy Spirit

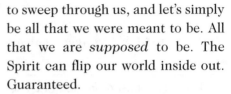

The most fertile, weed-free soil will not produce fruit unless it is first planted.

to sweep through us, and let's simply be all that we were meant to be. All that we are *supposed* to be. The Spirit can flip our world inside out. Guaranteed.

Notebook! Draw a picture of a tree with bare branches. You are going to set fruit in the tree. You have nine pieces of fruit: love, joy, peace, patience, kindness, goodness, faithfulness, gentleness, and self-control. The fruit that you set down low in the tree represent virtues that are easy for you. Fruit set in the middle represent the virtues you are working on, and the fruit up high represent virtues that seem out of reach for you. Go ahead and set your fruit.

Love

The love spoken of in Galatians 5 is *agape* love. *Agape* is God's love for us, a love, according to the *Evangelical Dictionary of Theology*, "that seeks to give, that seeks the highest good in the one loved, even though that one may be undeserving."

Agape love is always seeking what is best for the one loved, even when that love is unjustified (which is all the time). *Agape* love springs from the very essence of God, from His very nature.

When we invite Christ into our lives and become Christians, we take on a new nature. The Holy Spirit, who fills our hearts with light and grace, gives us the ability to say no to the old nature, the sin nature. This grace makes it possible for us to love as God loves, without expectation, without reward, and especially, without justification.

How hard loving can be at times! Yet that is what the cross is all about, and it is what I have received from Christ, who is incarnate love.

I know Him because He first knew me, and continues to know me. He knows me as a friend, one who loves me; and there is no moment, therefore, when His care falters. This is momentous knowledge.

J.I. PACKER

Notebook! Write a love note to God.

Joy

Paul tells us in Romans 14:17 that the very essence of the kingdom of God is righteousness, peace, and *joy*. Joy is an integral part of our relationship to God. It is far more extreme than giggles and gladness.

I look at it this way: Love and joy are paired closely because they are inseparable. Anyone who has ever felt the depth of true love knows what I mean. Regardless of your life circumstance, true love is unshakable. In fact, it sustains you. And you cannot contain your joy because of that love.

Think of joy as a bottomless feeling of contentment that comes from the love of God. When you have truly connected to the love of God—and fallen in love with Him—joy flows freely. When we connect with the profound sense of gratitude that comes from the staggering message of God with us, of redemption, and of eternity with Him, our joy is complete indeed.

Cana of Galilee...Ah, that sweet miracle! It was not
men's grief, but their joy Christ visited. He worked His
first miracle to help men's gladness.

FYODOR DOSTOYEVSKY

Celebrate!

Do you want to live a better life? Start living now with celebration. God shouts over us with joy—can we not return the favor? When we celebrate His bounty, we are honoring God and thanking Him. When we don't, are we returning His gifts unopened?

Bring this sentiment into your home and family. So what if all you have for dinner tonight is Scottish oats! Add raisins and brown sugar, draw a flag of Scotland, invent a family coat of arms, play a bagpipe recording, and lead your family in a parade. Joy is a distinct possibility in your life.

Modern Christianity generally has cut itself off
from both nature and culture.

WENDELL BERRY

Notebook! Write a poem to the tune of "Joy to the World" and title it "Joy in My World."

Peace

Many of us scream for peace in the world while ignoring our own inner scream for peace of mind, peace from stress, peace of spirit.

"Peace to you" we say with conviction, as we clasp the hand of pew sitters next to us on Sunday morning. "Peace and Joy" adorns the front of our Christmas cards. Peace, peace, peace. Inner peace, world peace, lasting peace, peace signs, peaceniks, peace treaties. It's even on bumper stickers.

Does anyone out there really believe we can have true and lasting peace without the intervening work of God the Holy Spirit?

The Holy Spirit goes beyond signs, cards, and bumper stickers. He transforms our lives from the inside out. Peace becomes a part of who we are, and it affects all of our relationships.

Peace I leave with you; my peace I give you. I do not give to you as the world gives. Do not let your hearts be troubled and do not be afraid.

JESUS

Patience

Patience: calming our expectations, slowing our drive, curbing our desire.

"Be patient!" we say to youngsters waiting for brownies to bake, for the movie to start, for Christmas morning to come. Wait. They will bake, it will start, and it will come. The prize is worth waiting for. Wait. You will get your reward. Be patient.

The Waiting Game

Isn't it interesting that patience is listed as a fruit of the Holy Spirit? Wait.

What are you waiting for? Weight loss? Financial solvency? How can God the Holy Spirit help you pass the time, get through the day, and keep your focus clear until you get that reward?

Enduring the Race to Your Goal

The word *patience* evokes the idea of endurance. Wait and endure. How do you do that? Where do we find the model? I think of endurance runners. I think of my sister Anne.

Anne runs. She just goes and goes. No flashy start, no grandstand cheers, just the lonely, endless *thud, thud, thud* of her shoes on pavement, often crossing her finish line with blistered and bloodied feet, chapped lips, and an aching body.

Hold it right there! Endurance is a gift? I'll just sit here and wave as she trots by.

Look at the analogy more deeply and personalize it:

You are in a race toward a finish line (a better life). The runner (you) enters the race (sets goals), trains (informs yourself), plans and plots your route (develops strategies), and actually looks forward to the race (mind-set).

Yes, you may become battered along the way, develop muscle cramps, and get tired. But you cross the finish line because of God's grace—and because of the gift of patience.

Be patient with everyone, but above all with thyself. I mean, do not be disheartened by your imperfections, but always rise up with fresh courage.

FRANCIS DE SALES

Notebook! Identify the area in your life where you most need to practice patience.

Kindness

In this bountiful harvest, kindness is the most social fruit that we have seen so far. Kindness is empathy toward the human nature of others around you. Kindness is generosity toward those less fortunate in material goods and in spirit. Kindness is humane treatment of the least of us and care for God's created order.

Kindness is the Good Samaritan; it is putting your creature comforts on hold to serve the poor and the needy; it is mercy. How *kind* our Lord has been to us!

"Thy loving-kindness," we sing in a popular hymn, is better. Better than anything I can come up with. "Thy mercy endureth forever," says the psalmist. "Blessed are the merciful," says Jesus, "for they will be shown mercy."

What does being merciful mean in your situation? Who are the people in your life to whom you must show compassion? Sensitivity? Understanding? Forgiveness?

This can be tough.

Listen—God knows your heart. He also knows your past, present, and future. A time may be coming when you will be better equipped to handle a renewed relationship, a confrontation, or true forgiveness toward someone who has wronged you. You must leave your heart in His hands and be willing to obey when the still, small voice of God whispers, *It is time. Make the call.*

Notebook! Ask yourself and your children every night, What kindness have you performed today?

Goodness

All men are born good, the saying goes. And I say *phooey*. If you want proof, monitor behavior as a child grows from an infant to a toddler. Where did the manipulative nature come from? The selfish demands? The hitting? The angry rebuke from the crib? From your attentive parenting and loving care? I rather doubt that.

There is good in all men. To me, that is more on the money. Why? Because we are all created in the image of God. That is pretty good! *Imago Dei.* God created us with inherent worth and dignity. This does not mean we share in God's nature—we aren't a bunch of little gods. But we *are* God's greatest creation.

Oh My Goodness!

The flip side of good is bad. Very few of us would consent to *that* moniker.

So if you're not bad, you must be good! Hmm... What attributes come to your mind when you think of goodness? I've come up with four: moral excellence, honesty, integrity, and purity. Does that list describe your character?

Notebook! How does *imago Dei* affect your effort to improve yourself today?

Faithfulness

Page after page, sentence after sentence, I've cited God's Word to encourage you, to awaken you, to prove to you that a better life is not only possible, but in a sense, a promise. Attach to that some very good news: God, according to the apostle Peter (and the rest of the Bible agrees) is not slack concerning His promises. He will not break a covenant. He will not waver. He will not lie.

He is faithful.

All the ways of the Lord are
loving and faithful.

PSALM 25:10

We can depend on God to keep His promises. Can other people depend on us to keep ours? Do we fulfill our commitments? Faithfulness, according to G.M. Burge, hallmarks the life of a Christian. Faithfulness to our Lord and to the covenant agreement He has made with us can be easily compared to faithfulness to others—a spouse, in particular—and to covenants we have made with them.

Faithfulness conjures thoughts of loyalty, steadfastness, reliability, dependability, and trustworthiness. How is your loyalty factor? The value of your word? Commitment to self and to others is also a hallmark in the life of someone trying to accomplish goals.

> *God is always with us; why should we not always be with God?*
>
> W.B. ULLATHORNE

Notebook! Pick a goal. Write a pledge.

Gentleness

Did you know Jesus said the meek are going to *inherit* the earth? It's kind of baffling: The unassuming wimp who lets others throw sand in his face ends up with the "earth"? Wait a minute! What "earth" are we talking about, anyway? The Western Hemisphere? The U.S.? Kansas? No. What it means is the "new earth" found in Revelation 21.

But what about the wimp? He's not quite who Christ had in mind. "The meek" of the Beatitudes refers to the *humble*. Humble, as in *humility*.

"By humility and the fear of the LORD are riches, and honor, and life," said Solomon (Proverbs 22:4 KJV).

Come to me, all you who are weary and burdened, and I
will give you rest. Take my yoke upon you and learn from
me, for I am gentle and humble in heart, and you will
find rest for your souls. For my yoke
is easy and my burden is light.

JESUS

Humble in Heart

Although I've mentioned that I cannot possibly come up
with a favorite Bible verse, one that ranks very high with me is
Micah 6:8: "He has showed you, O man, what is good. And
what does the LORD require of you? To act justly and to love
mercy and to walk humbly with your God."

Isn't that awesome? Yet what does walking humbly mean?
To be a milquetoast, a weakling, a doormat? To demean yourself in front of others? Is that how you think of Jesus, who
called Himself humble? Hardly.

Jesus gave us His most telling example of humility when He
washed His disciples' feet. Servants washed feet. In Matthew
and Mark, Jesus tells His disciples that He did not come to be
served but to serve.

Paul pipes in when he says, "In humility count others better
than yourselves." Why? To have a servant's heart, which was
modeled by the Master. That's why.

There is another reason to be humble. Once we connect
the dots we recognize that everything we have has come from
God's providence. We are nothing apart from His love, grace,
and mercy. God does not see us as CEOs, presidents, lawyers,
academics, mothers, fathers, writers, old, young, black, white,
American, Canadian, or Korean. He sees us only through

Christ's righteousness and sacrifice. That is humbling, regardless of how you cut the pie.

Notebook! Write out and memorize Micah 6:8.

Self-Control

Quick! What is the first thing that comes to your mind when you hear the word "willpower"? Denying yourself dessert? Refusing to smoke another cigarette? Not going back to that Internet site? It's all about controlling urges, isn't it?

Flip it inside out. Control of self. Fruit of the Spirit. Walking as a child of light. Stewarding your impulses. Hmm...

This is a biggie. Lack of restraint has a whole lot to do with diet and budget. (I can see this piece of fruit going higher and higher up your tree...)

Whenever the subject of our will enters the picture, it is easy to see that this is where we most need the intervening power of God the Holy Spirit. You either turn control of that self of yours over to God or you don't. Diet problems and financial problems are daunting...why go them alone?

The power of the flesh is so great that even in the Christian the will to do the will of God may be largely immobilized.

E.F. HARRISON

Spirit-Led Life

If only we could give over our lives to the complete control of God the Holy Spirit (*Lord, do with me as you wish!*) and then sit on the couch and not move. Wait for the lightning bolt, wait for the voice from heaven, and wait for the prize patrol to knock at our door. Doesn't work that way, does it? Rather, ask God to intervene and guide and counsel. Perhaps this can be accomplished through introspection and contrition.

Put aside time to commune with God. Take your Bible and your trusty notebook with you when you do. Give thought to your life: your habits, your history, your hurts, your health. Think about your inner self with honest reflection and offer contrition when necessary. Investigate the "why" of you, of who you are. Have you ever honest-to-goodness looked inside yourself? (I mean since the angst of your teen years.)

As you face issues, perplexities, uncertainties, sins and fears, hand them over. Give God the Holy Spirit an invitation to enter your life and tend the fruit He has already planted. Ask Him to bring a stepladder while you're at it, to help you reach the top of your tree.

Note from me: I've listed my "Ten Commandments of Fruitful Living" in the appendix.

The Tale of a Bad Day

Hubby-Dearest finally kicks in. In a particularly good mood because of his Thai indulgence, he volunteers to return the DVDs when he goes to fetch the take-out (and Missy), taking your car because his is low on gas. This frees you to spend quality time with Precious and Junior, and you plop them in the tub. A warm bath on such a cold night, some cocoa and cookies, and a story or two before their bedtime is much more important than straightening the house or putting this morning's laundry in the dryer. Except the laundry load was towels. You rummage through your hall linen closet to find clean towels in the disheveled mess and happily discover a pair of eyeglasses you lost months ago.

Once dried, your little angels curl into your lap while you balance a book and a cup of tea. The moment is idyllic: children, cozy chair, snow lightly dusting the outdoors, Pad Thai on its way, towels in the dryer...and Barky barfing on the Oriental rug.

Hubby-Dearest arrives with your oldest in a snit. "Up to your room!" he commands, and her door slams in response. You then learn that cellophane noodle soup—compliments of Missy's clumsiness—is marinating the floor of your car, making an interesting stew with those goldfish and pretzels.

Not having had dinner at her friend's ("They had eggplant lasagna! Gross!"), you heat a pre-packaged rice dish for Missy and invest yourself in conversation with her while Hubby-Dearest puts the others to bed—a *huge* nightly rigmarole. You eye the clock. You eye the brown bags filled with dinner. Missy talks on, informing you that she has (what else) a science project due in the morning, and she was selected to demonstrate the structure of an atom. The trouble is, the Tinkertoy set is in the bedroom with the finally quiet young ones.

Notions of a romantic dinner with your husband make way for eating out of cartons on a table swept partway clear of food debris, cereal bowls that smell of sour milk, the newspaper, and today's mail. Marshmallows, hard as rocks from sitting in an open bag since July 4 (two years ago), soda straws, and a soccer ball covered in crinkled aluminum foil that rips everywhere when you try to smooth it constitutes your family's rendition of atomic energy. One marshmallow bears the distinct stain of curry.

Utterly famished, the food you scarfed from cartons acti-vates your appetite alarm as you begin your evening ritual of "picking."

To be continued...

6
The 50 Percent Principle

This all started with a dog biscuit, so I guess I should thank our Lab, Jill, for what I consider a terrific concept. Like a moveable black rug, Jill follows me wherever I go. She is at my feet at this very moment as I write. At times, Jill will walk up, perch her big, blocky head on my lap, and turn those amber eyes of hers toward mine in supplication. This means one of two things: She needs to visit the outside, or (more likely) she wants a snack. (What's that they say about similarity between dogs and their owners?)

One day, after Jill performed this ritual, I obediently headed to the kitchen and reached into a big, colorful tin. In went my hand, and out came a large dog treat. While Jill sat and drooled, I summarily broke the biscuit in half. It's what I always do. For one thing, our vet says Jill will never know the difference, for another, breaking it in half means our dog biscuit purchase goes—hey!—twice as far. In other words, if we purchased one month's supply for, say, $5 (which we don't, this is just an example), we now have two months' supply. Here's another way to look at it: One month's supply now costs $2.50 instead of $5. A whopping 50 percent savings!

This is a great concept to introduce to readers, I thought as I tossed the half-biscuit in the air. The more I thought about the idea, the more excited I became.

Just Suppose

Suppose you could cut your caloric intake by up to 50 percent.

Suppose you could cut your expenses by up to 50 percent.

Would that help your overall bodily and financial health?

Here's a provocative thought: Suppose you could do all of that in a rather effortless manner by simply learning this 50 percent concept and bringing it into your life little by little? (In her broken English, my Polish grandmother would have said *lilla by lilla*.)

Lilla by lilla! I like that! Now you're cooking with gas! Is that what you are thinking?

You are out of your mind! Is that what you are thinking?

Reading about skills is one thing, introducing them into your life until they become automatic and effortless is another.

I not only believe it can be done but have been living this way for years. It took a moveable black rug named Jill to get me to connect my own dots and put a name to my system...a method to my madness, if you will.

I'm not suggesting that you can save 50 percent on your expenses by ten o'clock tomorrow morning (or at all, for that matter). What I am saying, and have proven to myself repeatedly, is that becoming adept with this principle will save you 50 percent on this, 30 percent on that, 25 percent, 15 percent, or 10 percent on nearly every expenditure. Your savings will match your skills.

Same with weight. I'm not suggesting that you can become a svelte runway model by tomorrow morning either. If you become adept with the practices I recommended—and develop your own strategies—you will drop a lot of calories here, a few calories there. Your caloric loss will match your application of these principles and your determination to apply them.

The 50 Percent Principle

I don't expect that *everything* you do should be or can be adjusted up or down by 50 percent. You can apply this principle in varying degrees. It all adds up in the end. You *can* nickel and dime yourself to financial health. You *can* nibble and sip your way to bodily health. And I will prove it to you.

> *Do not store up for yourselves treasures on earth, where moth and rust destroy, and where thieves break in and steal. But store up for yourselves treasures in heaven, where moth and rust do not destroy, and where thieves do not break in and steal. For where your treasure is, there your heart will be also.*
>
> JESUS

The 50 percent principle works like this: Pare down by percentages, build up by percentages. Fifty percent more or less: This principle can be applied to consumption, expenses, stress, and time. I dare say, once you understand it, you can apply the principle to most areas of life. Build up. Back off.

When Less Is More

The 50 percent principle applies to paring down overall weight and expenditures. By setting a goal to cut up to 50 percent off most of your expenses, your savings will increase. By setting a goal to cut up to 50 percent off most caloric intake, your waist will decrease.

Certain expenditures are fixed: Tithing and mandatory savings come to mind. I feel that just about every other expense is negotiable at some level. So how can you come up with more money by spending less? Here are just a few examples to whet your whistle:

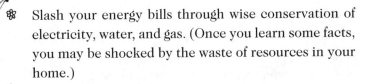

❀ Slash your energy bills through wise conservation of electricity, water, and gas. (Once you learn some facts, you may be shocked by the waste of resources in your home.)

❀ Learn the ins and outs of retail so you know when to get the best buys. Learn how to identify a good buy and where to shop.

❀ Organize your life (closets, car trunks, medicine cabinets, cupboards, freezer...) so you can avoid spending in the first place—and so that you use up to 50 percent less space.

Certain dietary requirements are fixed too: Vitamins and minerals come to mind. Without sacrificing nutrition, you can save calories by eating less of some things (and more of other things). Here are some examples:

❀ Learn to be satisfied with less.

❀ Learn to eat slower (and not shove wads of food into your mouth as if you were stoking the boiler on the *Titanic*.)

❀ Learn to chew your food more thoroughly.

When More Is Less

How can more be less? The 50 percent principle applies to building up too. A couple of financial examples:

❀ You can apply extra money you save (using this and other principles) to reduce high-interest consumer loans.

❀ You can use money you save to pay extra principle on your mortgage.

A few examples toward better health:

❀ Eat 50 percent more low-glycemic veggies.

❀ Walk 50 percent more.

❀ Drink lots more good, filtered water.

In some areas, cutting back expenditures or consumption makes perfect sense; in other areas it makes sense to increase. So let's talk about consumption.

Consumption

You've heard the message loud and clear from this book, from other books, from essayists, from radio personalities, and from your own conviction: We consume too much. Consumption applies to more than food. Sociologists use the term to refer to our use of material goods. That *stuff* again. How can we limit the amount of stuff we use? Hoo, boy! It will be hard for me to limit my *answer* to that question!

Stuff

Though this half of the book is dedicated more to reasoning than to doing, I will cite a few examples that might raise your consciousness:

❀ We dress from the top layers of our dresser drawers and from the easily accessible clothes stuffed in our closets. (Shall we say 25 percent of our clothes?) Stuff is stuffed everywhere, yet we run to the mall to buy more stuff, opting for trend over a personalized classic look. Get rid of 50 percent of the clothes in your home, and you will cut back stress, clutter, expense, strife, and time. In a *huge* way.

❀ We continue to purchase food while vast stores of food already in our house either languish in the cupboards, turn to slime in the fridge, or turn into ice crystals in the freezer.

Note from me: Statistics say the average American family throws one-half pound of food in the trash every day. Let's put an arbitrary value of $1 on that food. Hypothetically, that is $30 a month in the trash. Suppose your food budget is $200 a month. Fifteen percent of your budget, on average, goes in the trash.

❀ We are so disorganized that we shop regularly to replace articles we already have but can't find. One organization expert claims that 20 percent of our discretionary spending goes to replacement. (That sounds high, so let's cut it in half. Let's say 10 percent. It's no use—still stings.)

❀ We have to have the latest, no matter what. We have to impress others.

Note from me: I need to flip this one inside out. Will you please think about this? For the most part, you are trying to impress *total strangers* with how you look, what you drive, and where you live. *Total strangers* who themselves are clueless and could not give a hang.

Don't hoard treasure down here where it gets eaten by moths and corroded by rust or—worse!—stolen by burglars. Stockpile treasure in heaven, where it is safe from moth and rust and burglars. It's obvious, isn't it? The place where your treasure is, is the place you will most want to be, and end up being.

EUGENE PETERSON, *THE MESSAGE*

Food

Oh brudder. Where on earth do I start?

❀ We can't drive past those fast food places without being tantalized. *"And would you like to super-size your fries? It only costs a little more."* Let's suppose you spend $4 for your meal, and the add-on is 40 cents. Ten percent.

❀ Restaurants heap so much food into servings, the plates have to be reinforced with steel rods and cement. (I know these things.) The cost of buying these reinforced plates, I am sure, is passed on to you by increased prices.

> People aged 25 to 34 spend an average of 44 percent of their food budget eating out.

❀ We heap tons of food on our plates. Probably 25 to 50 percent more than we need to sate us. (I'm not talking about what we need to *sustain* us, because that would be extreme. I'm talking about what we need to fully, happily sate us. More on this later.)

❀ We can't drive anywhere without a cup of coffee or a latte. And super-size that too. In the meantime, we keep buying new to-go mugs. We either buy the new style and color on impulse when we're at the coffee shop, or we can't find the tops to the several hundred thousand mugs we now have.

Less Stress

Cut back 50 percent of my stress?! Friends for life, Cynthia!

Or maybe you're thinking, *No can do.*

It's really up to you.

I can offer skills galore, but until you master those skills and couple them with your mind-set and heart-set, you're going to be revving your engine but going nowhere. Bad, really bad, for the engine—kind of like most stress is bad, really bad, for the body.

If you are struggling with diet or budget, pretend for a moment that you are parked on a steep hill. And your car is a stick shift, no less. Until you learn to put that car in the right gear and develop the strength to pull back firmly on the parking brake, you may roll down the hill. Every single one of us has rolled downhill when learning to drive a stick shift. But we did learn, and now driving and parking are automatic and effortless.

So how can we apply the 50 percent principle to stress? I have no idea what the primary source of your stress is, but I'm guessing nonstop activity and too little time are factors. When we are stressed, we are unable to "get into gear," or to expend enough energy to properly steward weight or finances. We are too frazzled. (As I said, when I am up to my neck with deadlines, I eat like an idiot.)

Let's look at how we are affected by nonstop activity:

❋ Advances in communication have made some lives utterly miserable. Where once a note would come by mail and give us time to process its message before we responded, we now have instant text messaging. *Answer now! Make a decision now! Push the send button now!*

❋ Our country's dependence upon the automobile has contributed to our frantic pace of life. We once walked or took a city bus to our destination, but now we *must* drive for fear of getting clobbered by a passing motorist (who is so full of road rage he'd sue your heirs for the dent you made in his car). Malls, suburban sprawl, and streets impassable to pedestrians have put us behind the wheel 24/7.

❀ Children's activities have hit absurd levels. Sports, music, dance, Scouts, 4-H...no wonder we have to schedule *play* time for children. (That still sounds odd: Schedule *play* time for children...) So who runs ragged with all of this besides the kids?

❀ You have so much to do that you cannot possibly maintain order in your house or in your car or in your purse. Donna Reed, that model mother from the 50s, would be a blithering imbecile if she had to deal with your life. The ambulance crew would probably find her curled into a ball in the corner of her kitchen, drooling and murmuring something about her tuna casserole, as they came to take her away to a cozy, padded room.

Nickel and Dime Yourself to Financial Health

What do I mean when I say we can nickel and dime ourselves to financial health? Can't you just refinance the house to get out from under your debt load and be done with it? You can. A lot of people have, and in your case it might be a good idea. For some, however...

❀ Many older people are suddenly faced with repayment of home equity loans or a much later retirement date on their mortgage. How does that fly with plans for retirement?

❀ Many people opted for variable interest rates that were available when rates were at record low levels. With no cap built into the loan and with a change in rates in the future, what is the only direction the rates can go? Up.

❀ Many people refinanced and came up with money to pay their bills. Big deal. Just slapping their hand on the kitchen table and saying: "That's it! We're done getting into debt!" *does not work.* That kind of declaration has to have a strategy, along with skills and know-how to avoid unnecessary and brand spanking new debt.

Part 2 gives you countless tips to nickel and dime yourself to financial health. Here are a few:

❀ Once you learn that in most houses, if you leave the bathroom fan on for one hour you've depleted the entire house from most of its heat, you'll learn to switch off the fan.

❀ Once you learn that by buying bulk spices at the health food store you save a bunch of money over those small jars at the grocery market, you'll buy the bay leaves you need and pocket the change.

Nibble and Sip Your Way to Bodily Health

Why can't you just buy a book on the latest diet fad and lose weight like your friend did? You can. And the new plan may work for you just as well as it did for your buddy. For others…

❀ Once they lose the weight, they will put that latest book on the shelf next to all the others that helped them lose weight…for a while.

Slow down eating, speed up walking.

❀ Just like variable interest rates, their new weight, which they achieved through great sacrifice, will-power, and denial, has one direction to go if they abandon the program. Up.

- So they lost the weight by eliminating a long list of foods from their diet. Big deal. They miss some of those foods. (And, I might add, they should—I believe we are excluding too many important nutrients for the sake of a trim waistline.) Without strategy, skills, mind-set and heart-set, they may find themselves running out to buy the *next* book because they could not sustain such rigor.

Some examples of tips on nibbling and sipping:

- Once you really comprehend how critical water is to your overall health, you will gladly skip the drinks you pay money for and sip (hopefully filtered) water straight from your tap. Essentially for free.
- Some foods, such as apples, are much better for you in their whole, natural state, both nutritionally and for weight loss. Some people in the know have likened apple juice to soda pop...what are we giving our kids?

Proper Perspective Please!

Many of us become overwhelmed by the size of the task. For instance, look at your financial circumstance right now. Is it bleak? Is it more than you can bear to face? Does digging out of your predicament seem daunting or impossible? Suppose you just looked at the credit card account with the smallest balance? What if you made a pledge to pay that bill within a few months? Could you devise a strategy to come up with just that much extra money? Probably, yes. You might have to sacrifice and think creatively (more on that!), but the challenge of that one bill might not send you into the kitchen to drool alongside Donna.

Suppose you set a goal to exercise more. Rather than get all stressed about finding time to walk or jog, deliberately park a half mile from your office, or at least in the farthest spot in a parking lot.

Facing the big picture is necessary, but start with small percentages. Focus your goals on small, achievable projects first. Same thing with time.

In Good Time

One huge problem for us is our use of time. Proper perspective is critically important when applying the 50 percent principle to our time.

Time is not our mortal enemy. Time is part of God's created order. It is not bad, it is good. How we *use* time—just as how we *use* natural resources and our gifts—is the issue.

I am convinced that we have enough time to accomplish what we choose to. I have not wavered in this conviction throughout all of my years in the real world talking with real people. And my conviction comes from more than the old fiat that we "make time for what we want." One reason we don't make time or find time is that we are paralyzed by the overwhelmingly big picture. Do me a favor. If you are reading this in your home, take a gander. Look around you. Some of you may be looking at order. Some of you may be looking at clutter. For those of you who have difficulty getting a grip because the big picture paralyzes you, look at it this way: Focus on one area of your house or on one project that is important to you. And then do some math.

Do the Math!

The 50 percent principle is a numbers game. For instance, you have so much income each month and so much that you have to spend that money on. The conclusion is simple: Cut how much you have to pay, and you end up with more at the end of the month. Or you could make more money.

You may be able to make more money, you may be able to eat less food, you may even be able to control your stress, but you cannot make more time. You have 24 hours in each day.

I calculate that we allow, on average, seven hours each day for sleep. That leaves 17 hours or 1020 minutes in your waking day. Look at your day. *Big picture. Too much. Messy house. Can't cope.* Can you spare 1 percent?

Calculate 1 percent of 1020 minutes. I calculated it for you. One percent is a hair over ten minutes. Now pick a chore. Dedicate 1 percent of your waking hours to that chore. Here's an example:

Let's say you have a problem tidying your bedroom. Does a 1 percent investment sound doable for straightening up your bedroom in the morning? What kind of chores can you do in ten minutes?

Do a wall a day! Begin at a specific spot in your home and clean and organize your way around, following the wall. Take a year. Clean a small area each day. And if you don't get to it today, there's always tomorrow.

If you're smart and haven't tried to make your bed look as if it should be on the cover of *House o' My Dreams* magazine by covering it with dozens of foofy pillows, you will use—at the most—three minutes to make your bed. Yesterday's clothes on the floor? Underwear in the hamper, a couple of things hung in the closet, shoes in the shoe bag, sweater folded and returned to the plastic sweater bag...*maybe* three more minutes. Clear away the tea mugs and tidy the end tables: one minute, max. I suppose you could run a feather duster for about 30 seconds, but that's going over the top...hmm...three more minutes to spend...(sound of fingers tapping on my desk)...maybe you *could* add a few more foofy pillows to the bed.

Start Small

Start with 1 percent of your time. Invest your time in non-stop effort or spread it through your waking hours, but pledge to improve that one area of your life. Aim for easy percentages and work your way up as you progress.

What else could you give 1 percent of your day to? Two percent? Three percent?

What about giving some of your day to offering thanksgiving, to sitting quietly, to one cupboard in the kitchen, to one shelf in the linen closet, to writing a note to a friend, to reading a book on how to strategize...

Simply Skip

A variation to my 50 percent principle comes from strategies I have offered in a previous book. The variation is to *simply skip*.

Consider your daily treat at the coffee shop. This little treat of yours has become a routine expense. By skipping this expense every other day, you will cut your coffee shop expense in half. Can you skip other routine expenses (every other day or every other week) for significant savings?

Principles Galore

Part 1 will end with a review of important principles that have enhanced my life—and the lives of others—significantly.

In part 2 the rubber meets the road: Category by category, helpful hints will abound. Those hints will help you apply the 50 percent principle.

The Tale of a Bad Day

So tired your skin hurts, you pass on your pledge to clean your face with that fancy cream and don't even brush your teeth. You just want sleep. Hubby-Dearest is already far away in that nether-region men escape to the second their head hits the pillow—or the recliner, or the hammock for that matter. Though relieved that he is not in an amorous mood, you can't help but wonder if you are not looking young and desirable any longer. (When you shower, you notice that you're banging into body parts you didn't even know you *had*.) Becoming more alluring is one of the many promises you will make to yourself tonight. You do miss the spontaneity of love and touch. You smile when you look at the back of your husband's head, his bald spot becoming so much more obvious lately. No, you're not less desirable...you're both just dead tired.

Your mind wanders to what must be done tomorrow: Get up early to make a healthy breakfast for the family and take Missy and her project to school. You decide you can put work on cruise control for a while now that your presentation is over. There are the matters of your cocker escape artist, of trying to make a dent in your home tending, of clothes to sort through...

Driven not by guilt, but by sheer exhaustion, the old question rises again. Would life be better around here if you didn't work? You did stay home till Precious was one. And you do need the income. How you wish you could find a better way, a better life. This isn't what you thought your routine would be, even when you knew it would be a struggle.

You squint hard to look at the street light. Still snowing. The threat of no school tomorrow sends a shiver of anxiety through you. It wouldn't be the first time. You'll cope like you always do. And Hubby-Dearest isn't as slack as you make him out to be. You just feel so...*alone* at times. You feel as if all the responsibility is on top of you, grinding you into the ground. Relentless. But you've got big shoulders. You would not trade your life for the world. (Well, maybe parts of it...) Junior whimpers right on cue. You listen as he frets himself back to sleep, and you hear the soft sound of Barky's little tail as it wags against the carpeted floor. Hubby-Dearest flops over and his arm reaches across your body automatically, effortlessly. You stroke his arm as you doze off to sleep.

Good night, Lord Jesus, you whisper, as you have every night since you were a child, *I love you.*

The end of a bad day.

7
10 More Principles: A Primer

I'm not kidding when I say I've walked in pretty scuffed and worn shoes in the past. My story comes with drama, heartache, loss, and some tragic moments. I've also been a poor steward and a prideful servant. I let life carry me on its wave, on its terms, for long enough to find myself in dire straits. I tell you this because I want you to know that I get it: I know what it is like to be scared, to be suicidal, to be overwhelmed, and to be just plain clueless.

More than one factor brought me to where I am now. And I believe those factors have contributed to making me a much stronger person in this field of frugal living than I would have been otherwise.

I also know what it is like to want to lose weight, to feel ugly, and to wish I could "have the look" that everyone else has.

The factors that have helped me have certainly included finding faith in Christ and meeting and marrying Joe so long ago. Both were stabilizing events for me.

Over time, a latent ability toward resourcefulness and creativity began to surface. Once I coupled my own gifts in this area with what had been modeled for me as a youngster and what I learned from books and magazines, I was on my road to thrift. Even better, I was on my road to thrifty living with *style*.

With these skills in mind, I queried an editor and sold my first book. In that first book I enumerated 1001 ways to stretch a dollar. I also enumerated ten specific principles that guided me as I became more determined to succeed. (These ten principles are the entire focus of my most recent book, *Living Well on One Income.*)

Part 2 will summarize much of what was in that first book and add much more. I hope learning these ideas will be as fun for you as revisiting them was for me.

In this short chapter, I want to briefly highlight my ten principles for your success. If you are already familiar with these strategies, consider this a refresher course. If you are new to them, consider this a primer.

Number One: Roll Up Your Sleeves

If you are intent to live a better life, you are going to find yourself on the business end of a garden hose as you wash your own dog or car, on the business end of a French knife as you chop your own lettuce for salad and slice your own cheese, and on the business end of an iron as you press your own shirts.

To live a better life, you will ask what you can do yourself that you normally pay someone to do for you. You will cook your own, pump your own (unless you're in Oregon or New Jersey), sew your own, and grow your own. Not fanatically, just sensibly.

You will also put effort into caring for what you have so you don't have to replace or mend or fix your belongings more than necessary. You will bend over and gather something underfoot; you will empty trash from the car when you gas up, you will put that cream on your face, if only by keeping it on the nightstand and smearing it on as you nod off to sleep.

I'm mentioning the "work" principle first to get it out of the way. Don't be put off by this and don't be intimidated. I'm not one of those who think you should be making your own soap or spinning your own wool. That would put undue stress on you and be unrealistic. I am saying that if you are serious about your intent to manage your weight or your finances, you're going to have to put some elbow grease and effort behind your conviction.

Number Two: Organize Your World

This is probably as pleasant as talking about sin. Aw, come on, it's not that bad. A real, no-kidding truth is behind this principle: An ordered life is not only a better life, it is a weight program with more chance of success and a checkbook with more money in its balance.

Organization is the bedrock on which you build success. As I mentioned before, through organization you are aware of what you have and are less inclined to purchase duplicate items. You are also more inclined to use what you already have (my favorite principle!). You are also happier.

Don't tell me you like coming home to a messy house. I won't believe you. I am not talking perfection. I am not talking eat-off-the-floor clean. I am *not* talking Donna Reed! I am talking about having such a sense of care and gratitude for your body and your belongings that you do your utmost to keep them well.

Purple Rhinoceros

Good. I have your attention. So listen:

A recent report by the nonprofit group Children and Adults with Attention-Deficit/Hyperactivity Disorder claims that up to 4 percent of our adult population, including some four million women, suffer from this problem. The Center for Adult ADHD recently acknowledged that only 40 percent of children outgrow their disorder, meaning 60 percent or so will continue to have these symptoms late in life. A study by the University of Maryland claims that parents of ADD/ADHD children (especially mothers) are 24 times more likely to have the disorder themselves. If you really, really can't get a grip, maybe you should talk with your doc.

Number Three: Use Things Up

Alrighty then: We're talking Jell-O in the kitchen cupboard. Let's use that tiny box of sugar and flavoring to make a point. Why is Jell-O still sitting in your cupboard from a couple of years ago? Is it some precious heirloom? A dessert specialty so remarkable that you are saving it for your daughter's wedding reception? So excruciatingly hard to make that you are waiting for a three-day weekend so you can tackle it?

Or did you decide several years ago that you were going to begin a new hobby: Jell-O stashing. Or maybe you thought it would be fun to go out and spend money (of which you claim you don't have much) so you could bring things home and put them in your cupboards. I get it. Sort of a Jell-O deco. Which is why every now and then, especially when you think you've hit a sale, you buy *more* Jell-O! Just like the meat in your freezer, the tools in the shop, and the hair conditioner in your bathroom.

Use things up. Most of us could feed our families for weeks on end with what we have on hand. And write a million letters. And burn a hundred candles. And wear a different outfit every day. And have the shiniest hair on the planet.

Number Four: Waste Not

This principle cuts to my heart, so I will cut right to the chase.

Many times, in person or on radio, I've been asked by sincere people how to save money—for a variety of reasons. This question always pops up during the holiday season. Are you asking that question right now? Please don't think me cruel to ask a question in return. Do you throw food in the garbage?

How can you *begin* to save if you are throwing things away? It is counterintuitive. And it has to strike at the heart of God: *I don't really care about the blessings I have, Lord, and I don't really care about the plight of others. I don't like this (food, blouse, game, book, whatever), so I'm pitching it out. Don't waste!*

And don't forget that waste comes with many faces: food, utilities, sunsets, your gifts, your freedom, and friends.

Number Five: Discover Your Creative Genius

Another way to put this is to look for the path of least expenditure. If you are facing a costly purchase or repair or payment of any kind, sit back and brainstorm. What can you do to save money? Let me give you a quick example.

We live with our son and his family in Virginia on and off during the winter months, and we walk extensively since their house is close to the city center. Jill, our Lab, is not accustomed to spending much time outdoors during extremely cold weather. The cold became too much for her. I knew I could buy a dog coat for her for $30. Did we have the money? Yes. But creative genius automatically kicked in: *Hmm... where can I find something that will work as a dog coat?* Shazam! To the Goodwill store I went, where I found a child's polar fleece jacket with a zipper in front, and elastic around the waist. Fits Jill to a tee. Even sports Michael Jordan's #23 on it. $1.29. She is the hit of the downtown crowd. A real slam-dunk.

Number Six: Live Within Your Means and Learn Prices

Both halves of this principle are equally important. You have to know what your "means" are in order to live within them, and you should know reasonable prices for things you normally buy. That way you will know when you hit a good sale. You will also know whether the Sale o' the Century that you stumble upon is bona fide or just a markdown after a ridiculous markup. In other words, know how much going to the cleaners costs so you don't get *taken* to the cleaners.

Watch store clerks ring up your item. I have "caught" well-intentioned (and sometimes harried) store clerks running items through twice, and I have caught scanner errors—especially when sale items have not been keyed into the computer.

Be careful to count your change, as well, when you purchase with cash.

Knowing your prices also includes knowing the interest rates you pay on different accounts—and doing something about them if you can.

Number Seven: Presentation Is Everything

Presentation is all about celebrating the bounty of life that God has given to you.

Look—you will have dreary days. We all do. Presentation is not about acting like a fool in the face of dire times, or running around barefoot in the snow, claiming to be having a swell time building a snowman.

Presentation is living life with gusto, setting a fun table, throwing open your door and your heart to friends, and sharing the last morsel you have with them...on a silver platter. Presentation is (yes, Sheila) furniture placement, wildflowers you picked for free, or bare branches in a tall glass vase. And (yes, Mom) it is finally wearing that scarf that's been in your closet all this time, to bring attention upwards—because you have such a pretty face.

Number Eight: Adjust Your Attitude

If you do not have the right attitude, you are going to sink your ship quicker than a cannonball from the SS *Doomsday*. Attitude makes or breaks you. Attitude *defines* you! This is where contentment comes into the picture. As Paul told his protégé, Timothy, "godliness with contentment is great gain." Contentment, trust, joy—they spring from faith.

A right attitude means that you have chosen to courageously face your situation out in the open, to confront your circumstance head-on, whether by opening your mail and totaling your bills, or looking in a store window at your reflection. And if you have a right attitude and see that something needs doing, you will do something about it.

Number Nine: Out with Impulse

Statistics tell us that 50 percent of what we buy, we buy on impulse, and 25 percent of what we buy, we don't even need. Notice how positively *crammed* the checkout area is becoming with impulse items. Lots of money, boardroom talk, and reasearch went into determining what you would most likely buy. Merchandisers have actually figured out that if you pick up an item, you are 50 percent more likely to purchase it! Talk about the 50 percent principle!

Will you occasionally see something that jogs your memory and reminds you that you need it? Of course you will. Happens all the time. That is not impulse. Impulse is when you walk into Shoptilyoudrop with no purchase in mind—until your eyes lock onto *it*. Must have. Cold sweat. Cart home. Put down. Right there on your shelf. You never touch, use, smell, burn, wear, or soak in it, but it's there.

Number Ten: Honor God

Though I have already talked about this, I have decided to quote directly from my first book for an attitude that I feel cannot be improved upon. Here is what I wrote in 1995:

> We made a rule in our home long ago: We do not allow any thing, any behavior, any speech, any music, any video, or any TV show that would hurt

the heart of our holy God or blaspheme His holy name. We try hard to abide by this rule. (Note in 2004: We still try hard.)

The Bible tells us we are to be in the world but not of it. Being in the world is a real challenge. The world is filled with allure—it beckons us to buy happiness, beauty, success, popularity, and contentment.

King Solomon said in Ecclesiastes 5:10, "Whoever loves money never has enough; whoever loves wealth is never satisfied with his income."

Never let the love of things or your quest for a certain lifestyle rob you of your first love, the Lord Jesus Christ.

That is a good attitude, indeed. It is also a good way to end the first part of this book, as a reminder of our focus and of our call to walk as children of light as we live a better life to the honor and glory of God.

Part Two

The How of It

Introduction to Part Two

How *Do* You Do!

If I did my job in part 1, you will read the rest of this book with a somewhat different insight than you had when you began. You may now welcome hints and suggestions into your life because they jibe with a deeper worldview and perspective. I hope you now have a determination toward better stewardship and a greater understanding of "why."

Part 2 should be fun. In part 2, I address areas of life that affect you the most. This half of the book includes a happy mix of advice and tips I've learned from others, along with several of my own.

Here are some headings to watch for:

❋ *Go to the Pro!* In these sections, I share information from professionals, merchants, and service folk about how we can save money by buying or using their products.

❋ *Tag Along!* Here I bring you into my daily routine.

❋ *Try This!* Look for simple plans of action.

❋ *Stopwatch!* These sections include time-saving tips.

❋ *50 Percent!* And, of course, I apply the 50 percent principle to budget and to diet.

DITCH the Diet

In part 1 I used the word *DITCH* to encourage you to Deconstruct any negative patterns and thoughts, to Inform yourself so you will be better equipped to deal with financial issues, to never stop Trying to succeed with money management, to consider how rampant Consumption has become, and to care about overall Health.

Most of us need to deconstruct our thinking about our bodies. The message the world sends us nonstop is that thin is in. The health crowd has made sensible attempts to encourage us to trim our body fat, but let's get real. With few exceptions, merchandisers use pretty, skinny models (or models that are pretty skinny) as cultural icons when peddling products. They suppose we are vapid and vain enough to believe that buying their product will make us look just like those models. DITCH that nonsense! We should all carry a healthy weight. Period.

Here is my blunt and honest opinion. I have learned that we are complete idiots about proper nutrition, that we do not eat properly to fuel and support our body's phenomenally intricate organ functions, that we live in a chemical soup, that we *eat* chemical soup, that our immune systems are suppressed, that we live in abject fear of cancer and Alzheimer's, that diabetes is soaring sky-high, and that for the most part, we do not have vitality or robust health. This is not living a better life. This is *nuts*. If you agree with me, it's up to you to get a grip, DITCH the diet, and do something about your health once and for all.

DITCH the Budget

I earnestly hope that you become so adept at DITCHing the budget that stewardship becomes automatic.

❀ You've learned to control the impulse factor in your life and have begun to use what you have. Because of this, you gradually wean yourself from shopping for shopping's sake. Because of that, you have a bigger balance in your checkbook.

❀ You've learned to care for what you have and you settle for driving an older car even though desire to replace that clunker can seem irresistible. By keeping your car serviced, rotating your tires, and not driving with your foot on the brake anymore, you've cut back wear and tear. Even though you face repairs every now and then, when you consider new car payments, you know you are ahead of the game. And your auto insurance and license plate costs are lower.

❀ By facing your financial predicament head-on and tackling high interest rates on your consumer accounts, you've alerted yourself to where your money goes and have made a conscious choice to crave less stress rather than more things. As a result of that, little by little (*lilla* by *lilla*), you savor the sweet success of small victories, which far outweighs and outlasts any momentary pleasure that comes from the gimme-gotta-haves.

8
The Significant Matter of Others

Of the many factors to consider whether trying to lose weight or to save money, the input of other people matters—and is one example of the benefits of living alone (no one can sabotage you). But situate yourself in a home environment that has just one more person, or add finicky little munchkins to the equation and then try to have success. Might be easier to join my sister Anne as she runs over boulder fields before breakfast. So let's talk about other people and getting them on board. How do you get others to go along with your newfound view and perspective?

Communicating with your husband, parents, children, friends, and coworkers is a critical skill. I dare say many of us have not thought much about this skill, nor have we become terribly adept. Rather, we go through life butting heads, getting hurt (that would be me), turning sullen, crying, giving the silent treatment (that would also be me), storming out, becoming resigned, waiting for the ice to break, and getting along for a while. Then we butt heads again.

I heartily encourage you to consult the books and advice of those who are trained and knowledgeable in the area of interpersonal relationships. What I offer here is a brief treatment of communication skills as incentive for further investigation on your own.

If you read my book *Living Well on One Income,* you are familiar with the principle of ownership. I explain this principle by encouraging shoppers to give store managers, merchants, and service people a stake in the shopper's purchase or need for service.

❀ If you are trying to save money buying a computer, ask the computer store personnel to *help* you buy a computer and save money.

❀ If you are looking for a lower interest rate, instead of asking the credit card company for a reduced rate, ask *how to go about* getting a reduced rate.

Ask, ask, ask. Get other people to invest thought and help find a solution; give them ownership in a team objective. Same principle with people close to you, especially when you're dealing with weight loss and finances. So let's start with giving ownership to that all-important "other" in your life: your husband. I've invented a few scenarios just for fun.

Scenario Number One

You are all aflutter with enthusiasm and can barely wait for Hubby to walk through the door so you can share your thoughts with him. Hubby is up to his hair follicles with stress over a turn of events at work and thinking only of making it through the door.

The "conversation" goes like this:

You: "Iamsoexcited! Starting tomorrow we are turning over a new leaf! No more sugar, no more white flour, no more red meat, no more whole milk. No pasta, no rice, no pretzels, no ice cream. You get to go along with this, Bub, and you better not complain. We're going to lose weight, and we're going to save money. Water! That's it! Pack water for lunch. And breathe. Breathing is okay. On odd-numbered days. Go get that

big garbage can—I'm throwing all this junk out of the fridge.
And your sock drawer...we have to organize! We'll start there.
And you know those golf clubs you couldn't live without? The
ones you never use? Use it or lose it, Buster! We're on our way
to better living!"

Note from me: I'll tell you where you're on your way
to...and it certainly isn't better living. Right now, you're headed
for the inevitable argument.

Hubby: "What are you so worried about! We pay our bills,
don't we? And you're perfect just the way you are!" (Or Hubby
may say, "You do your own *@!# diet and leave my socks
alone!")

Some sort of built-in resistance usually kicks in when one-
half of a marriage makes a decisive declaration for change.
Maybe it's human nature, or maybe it's gender related. For
instance, if I say black, for some crazy reason, Joe senses his
bounden duty to say, "Well, maybe a shade of gray...hmm....
Actually, white...."

Maybe this has something to do with that "variety is the
spice of life" business. So how do you announce your new leaf
when you are expecting resistance? Ownership. Try something
like this:

Scenario Number Two

You are all aflutter with enthusiasm and can barely wait for
Hubby to walk through the door so you can share your
thoughts with him.

Hubby is up to his hair follicles with stress over a turn of
events at work and thinking only of making it through the door.
He's glad you give him time to transition and play with the kids
in order to zone out for a while.

You: "Hey, Man o' My Dreams, I've been struggling with
worry about my weight and about our finances. I really could
use some advice." (You're asking him to ride up on his white

steed and help you, telling him what the issues are in advance and showing respect for his opinion.) "Do you think we could take a walk around the block around seven?" (You're not ambushing him with any issues now, and you're not posing a threat because seven is a good two hours before his favorite TV show.) "I'm really hoping you can give me some pointers." (You are not asking to *talk*. "Talk" frightens the tar out of men. "Pointers" is different. It's direct and, well...to the point.)

Later, at seven...

Man o' Your Dreams: "Yeah, so what's this all about? Do I have to give up meat?"

You: "The last thing I want to do is sound selfish, but I'm really at my wit's end about this. I've given this a lot of thought, and I've tried to inform myself so I don't end up running down a dead-end road. Let me tell you what specifically worries me." (Fill in the blank). "Do you have any suggestions?" (In a perfect world, he will have a suggestion besides "I don't know," or "Do I have to give up meat?")

You, continued: "I get your point." (Be prepared. You might get smacked over the head with a two-by-four if he gets a chance to *really* tell you how he sees it.) "Let me tell you what I've been thinking and reading, and you tell me what you think." (Go from there.)

In *Living Well on One Income,* I encourage couples to hold regular meetings to discuss all aspects of their marriage relationship. These meetings should be regular, away from home's distractions, and followed by "review" meetings. Baseball bats, clubs, and boxing gloves are strictly verboten.

I feel most men will be amenable to a conversation that does not come across as an ultimatum. Some gruff fellows remain out there, however. In past books, I've joked that if you have a complainer on your hands and, for instance, have to have cereal for dinner because of budgetary constraints, stick a meatball in his corn flakes. For some women, this is not a joking matter. The determination to succeed with weight control or money management may have to be yours alone. If that's the case, don't forget prayer.

Father in heaven, guide my actions, guide my thoughts, guide my choice of words. Help me to express my sincere desire for sound stewardship in a manner that is understandable and non-threatening. Please prepare my husband's heart and mind for this dialogue. In Jesus' name I pray. Amen.

Talking with My Husband Is Child's Play... What About the Kids?

Fair warning: I am old-fashioned and doubtless out of touch with child-rearing practices of the twenty-first century. And I made big-time mistakes with Joshua. But I do have some thoughts on the matter of children.

I dig kids. I believe that children are more capable of understanding and cooperating with certain issues than we give them credit for. I also feel that children should be shielded from much of the stress that inhabits daily life. We should relate to children on an age-appropriate level. But (here it comes...) I do not believe children should be babied.

On one hand, we demand excellence and expect children to outperform every other child in the country in sports, the arts, or academics. (I cannot *begin* to tell you how relieved we are that our grandchildren aren't pushed beyond their interests...which are fickle and few at their age.)

On the other hand, we tend to allow children's primal, selfish demands to go unchecked. Children need structure and they need parameters. As the adult, your assignment is to provide that security and stability with the wisdom of Solomon.

Structure does *not* mean rigid schedules and unbending rules. If children are hungry, feed them. (But feed them intelligently, please.) If a child messes up, bend a little. Children are part of our families, and we should treat them as such. Children of all ages need to learn how to participate in age-appropriate family meetings that incorporate everyone's views. Proverbs 22:6 tells us to "train a child in the way he should go, and when he is old he will not turn from it." You are the one to teach your children skills so that when they are old they will profoundly benefit from them and thank you for them. One such skill is thrift, or sound money management. The other is establishing healthy eating habits.

Let's look at both categories briefly, from a parent's point of view.

Finances

Kids are an expensive proposition, and demands on the pocketbook are relentless. Here are a few suggestions that might be helpful:

❀ *Find and press the mute button during TV commercials.* Many of us carefully monitor what our children watch on TV, and along come distasteful, violent, and immoral promotions for movies, not to mention ads selling everything from Sugarfrostedfluffio's to women's seductive underwear. (When Joe and I watch TV with our grandchildren, we not only mute commercials, but also occasionally distract the kids.)

❀ *Set limits immediately.* Giving way to your children's every desire spells disaster for them in later life. Teach your children the abundance of a simple, godly life. Should you buy that "I'll *die* if I don't get it!" outfit or CD? It's up to you, but if you do, buy it in a way that does not give the child a sense of entitlement. Perhaps a chore, a specific accomplishment, or a real effort to control behavior can be incentive for the treat. Do not deny everything! Nothing is wrong with treating your child to something he or she wishes for once in a while. They *are* children!

❀ *Define financial limitations to your kids.* I'm borrowing liberally from my book *Money & Me,* where I encouraged parents to assemble bills and a notebook and convene a family meeting when no one is hurried. Maybe over pizza. The purpose of the meeting is to demonstrate the relationship between your income and your expenses. Use dollar bills and coins—or beans—to illustrate. Break it down specifically: "I have to work three hours in order to buy you a pair of shoes." Assure the kids that you are providing for them and will continue to do so. Do not scare them. Ask them what they think they could do, individually or together, to cut back on their expenses or to save. Provide incentive for good results, such as a "recreation" or "vacation" jar to collect savings.

❀ *Use age-appropriate language and have age-appropriate expectations.* Ultimatums are sometimes necessary with children. Rigidity, however, is not. "We don't do that," or "My way or the highway," or the classic "When you are old you can [fill in the blank]" may not be respectful of your children's emotional and physical needs. (I chuckled to myself when our son admitted, "Mom, I swore I'd never say 'Because I said so!' when I had children...and now I say it all the time!") Simply crossing your arms and slamming your foot might create hurt and rebellion in your kids.

*Fathers, do not exasperate your children;
instead bring them up in the training and
instruction of the Lord.*

EPHESIANS 6:4

✾ *Give an allowance.* Decide whether or not you wish
to pay your children for chores they perform at home.
(We did not believe Josh should be paid for doing his
fair share in the family, but we did offer him a "bonus"
when he did something extra.) Make a list of items the
child is fiscally responsible for. These might include
such things as movies, video rentals, snacks, a school
lunch, school supplies, clothes, savings, and gifts. I read
about one smart mother whose son asked to live at
home after graduation. The rent? The son was responsible for the family's electric bill. I'm guessing that poor
family stumbled around in the dark soon after.

Tag Along!

I have never purchased a toy for any of our grandchildren,
and I probably never will. That is not because I do not love
them, nor is it because I am some mean tightwad. (See The
Creed in the appendix.) They simply already *have* toys. Anything I bought would be redundant at best. Joe and I have gone
out of our way, however, to spend lots of time with our grandchildren. We have also decided that the best gift we can give is
a sense of financial stewardship. (This is in sync with what
their parents teach them.)

When the eldest, Ellen, turned four, we decided to give her
an "allowance" of $4 each week. We selected four matching

plastic jars to serve as banks and labeled them: Church, Other People, Savings, and Ellen. We have a ceremony on Friday afternoons when she deposits 40 cents in both Church and Other People, 70 cents in Ellen, and the balance into Savings. She knows that the Church money must go with her on Sunday mornings. She knows that the Other People money must be spent on behalf of the less fortunate, and she has already selected a local charity. She knows that once money goes into Savings *it does not come out,* and she knows that money marked Ellen is for her use.

Our intent is to give her a weekly allowance that matches her age. (Yes, we've thought about a cap!) With the help of adults, Ellen has met with a financial consultant and has begun a diversified savings portfolio, which should provide a lovely nest egg for her as she begins college. That makes way more sense to us than giving her another stuffed animal.

Food

As you think about your children's diet, remember that more is at stake than nutrition. Consider the matter of the parent-child division of authority. You are the parent—so be one. Many parents fall back on a couple of popular notions these days:

1. Pick your battles.

2. Kids somehow grow up even if they don't eat a balanced diet when they are young.

Keeping in mind that I am not a child psychologist and that a child psychologist might very well say that I'm full of prunes, let me offer my opinion on those two statements.

1. Why is proper discipline (and in a huge sense, *discipling*) of children called a battle? Who on earth

reduced our relationship with our kids to that kind of language? For one thing, though children will test you and use their personalities and wiles on you, *you* are the parent. Telling Missy or Junior to eat a child-friendly meal that does not contain revolting foods is not a battle. It is a parent telling a child to eat dinner. And it is an order, not a supplication. (Kids will let you know what is genuinely revolting: Josh would not eat squash or tomatoes.)

2. Kids may be growing up all right, but they are growing up fat and predisposed to diabetes, and they have the attention span of a gnat. Here are some suggestions:

   ☆ Do not be too rigid here either. A child should have some leverage and some bargaining power.

   ☆ Take children shopping every now and then and explain the value of fruits and veggies. Learn about selection and seasonal availability together.

   ☆ Hide the chopped kale (and other healthy foods) in soup, casseroles, or spaghetti sauce.

   ☆ Get the kids in on making the meal by giving age-appropriate and safe tasks.

   ☆ Make the food inviting. Turn egg frittatas into funny faces, layer yogurt and natural jams in a parfait glass, or build a "haystack" out of brown rice and surround it with a forest of barely steamed broccoli.

   Note from me: Be sure the broccoli has a bit of real butter or good olive oil...fats help with vitamin A absorption.

   ☆ Talk with your children. Read to them about healthy foods. Teach them to read labels or to listen as you read labels in the store. Our son and daughter-in-law read a child-level book about vegetables to rapt attention.

Tag Along!

When Joshua was three, he went to the grocery store with one of my friends. As she wheeled him down the cereal aisle, he screamed in terror (and for all to hear), "This is the junk aisle! Somebody save me!"

His comment was a little extreme, but I was not a big believer in cereals for breakfast. When Joshua was young, we did not have the wonderful choice of healthy and organic cereals we have now. We just began hearing about granola! Anything puffed and processed and sugared is not high on the nutritional scale. (Why do manufacturers have to *add* vitamins and minerals? Why did they process them *out* in the first place?) Anything puffed and processed, even if not sugared, tends to spike the glycemic index. Bad news for your pancreas. If not balanced with other foods, processed cereals for breakfast play a part toward predisposition to diabetes. Not to mention the morning slumps and grumps.

Try This!

All right...so you are not going to relinquish the cereal, partly because it is handy in the morning when you're trying to keep all the ends together. How do you add nutrition and cut costs? (I've read that the cereal aisle is the most expensive in the market. The average difference in brand name and generic products is more than 50 percent.)

❀ Find colorful, pourable containers for each family member. Turn the kids loose with permanent markers and stickers, and tell them they are decorating *their very own* cereal container.

❀ Transfer their "gotta have" cereal to the container.

❀ After a few weeks, buy some of the bulk or generic cereal that mimics their favorite, and mix it with the favorite in equal parts. Do this when the kids are not in the kitchen.

❀ Try to make the added cereal one that is high in fiber and low in processing. Add chopped raw walnuts, almonds (Careful! Choking hazard!), sunflower seeds, and pumpkin seeds.

❀ Chunks of apple would be great too, either chopped small and in the cereal (probably pushing your luck there) or sliced and served separately.

❀ Make a rule: No switching to a different type of cereal until the container is empty.

As a bonus, you get rid of all those pesky boxes that don't fit well in the cupboard anyway. Did you know that groceries are usually more expensive when they come in boxes, instead of bags? And look where bags of cereal are sold in the store—bottom shelf, right? Most expensive items are eye level. I guess the store figured out that you won't bend over to select something. Fool them. And give yourself 50 percent more exercise when shopping.

9
Food Stuff

I watch what some of you put in your shopping carts at the grocery store. And I see lots of your cars in the wrong grocery store parking lots.

I know what's in your cupboards (and in that cosmic black hole you call the freezer). No, I really do—for a time I cleaned homes for a living. I *know* what you grow in your fridge and what you throw away.

And I can usually tell what you eat just by looking at you or at your children.

Food for Thought

Man may not live by bread alone, but the simple truth is that we can't live without food. I put food first in this section because I am certain that in this murky area we have much to learn, much to change, and *so much* to save! I have not an iota of doubt that the average person can effortlessly cut 25 to 50 percent off the monthly food dollar, and I'm going to show you how.

> Let food be your medicine and medicine be your food.
>
> HIPPOCRATES

I also have no doubt in my mind that you can have your cake and eat it too. Sassy as I may be at times, I am on your side. I want to

139

make things easier for you. The whole concept of this book is to help you attain a better life!

Can you grind your own beans, use good olive oil, go to a restaurant every now and then, and still save money on food? Absolutely. I've been doing it myself for years!

Can you eliminate processed foods that are high in sugars, salts, trans fats, hydrogenated fats, and "natural flavors" without losing the joy of eating and without feeling underfed? Beyond a shadow of a doubt. I finally figured that out too, though it took me years!

I'm dividing "food" into three categories: buying, keeping, and eating. Volumes of information are available, but I'll just give you the most helpful tips.

Food, The Buying of

Remember when your grade school teacher explained the concept of who, why, when, where, what, and how? Let's apply that to shopping for groceries. The "who" is you, and I think we've already given enough attention to "why." So now we're on to...

When to Shop for Food

Since I've shifted from the philosophical to the mundane, I am going to offer practical measures that effectively deal with when you should shop. In a perfect world, you would shop...

❉ When you are not hungry. (Eat an apple before you shop. It is low on the glycemic index and will keep you filled long enough to get in and out without mugging the poor old man handing out cheese samples.)

❉ When you are alone, unless you are bringing the children for a shopping lesson. It's true—shop with children or shop with a friend and you'll spend more money.

❀ When you are not stressed. (Remember, this is in a perfect world.) Early hours or late hours tend to be less stressful. Factor seasonal crowds at the market too. Have you ever gone to a warehouse store a few days before Christmas? Might as well pack a lunch and bring your sleeping bag! Crowds spike at other times of the year too: before a big storm, before the Super Bowl, and on Labor Day weekend.

❀ When your shopping list reaches "it's time" status. I discourage routine grocery shopping, especially since I am so gung ho on using what we have on hand. My system? Use things up! Unless they are necessary items (such as diapers, milk, bread, and produce), merely add an item to your master list and go without for a while. If you use the last of your soy sauce, go without soy sauce until your shopping list hits *tilt*. Quit running to the market on a hit-and-miss basis. Might as well be playing the slots in Vegas.

Stopwatch!

Save time by shopping during off-hours, using a list, and sticking to your list. (Buying something that's not on your list isn't a felony. Just be sure it's a wise purchase. Potato chips for the ride home is not what I have in mind.)

Shop Seasonally

Eating seasonally is less expensive and healthier, and a regional and seasonal diet puts us more in harmony with our world. Maybe a *tiny* part of why we feel out of sync with life is because we have abandoned some of the natural rhythms that once balanced us. Thanks to technology and the all-night phenomenon, we are no longer in step with our circadian rhythms. What do I mean? We don't sleep at night according to our

design. We don't rest on the Sabbath according to the commandment. And we don't eat foods that are fresh from the rich
earth and still filled with vitality as we were supposed to. We get
our grapes from Chile.

Shopping seasonally is particularly frugal and adds tremen-
dously to the enjoyment of food:

❊   Once we looked forward to the early spring asparagus
     crop and scouted recipes in our (sigh) trusty cookbook.

❊   Once we could not *wait* for strawberry shortcake or
     strawberries and cream. They were treats and sure
     signs that summer was here. A sign of the season.

Seasonal food sales mean more than fresh fruits and veggies. Certain times of year present good bargain opportunities
for the consumer. Develop the habit of buying seasonally for
the nutrition of fresh (and local!) food—and for the economic
advantage.

Let me ask you this: When do you eat pumpkin pie? Why
only then? I'll tell you why: Food plays a ritualistic role in the
seasonal rhythm of life. Pumpkin pie just isn't the same on the
Fourth of July. It has meaning, purpose, and a deeper signifi-
cance at Thanksgiving than just another dessert on the table.

Go to the Grocery Pro!

❊   Holiday demands in particular cause vendors to com-
     pete with each other for your attention.

❊   Turkeys are loss leaders that draw customers to stores.
     A store may pay 79 cents a pound and sell the turkey for
     39 cents a pound. Get your turkeys *before* Thanksgiving;
     they will shoot up the day after. And be alert to condi-
     tions stores now put on their loss-leader purchases. If
     you are stocking up, ask the butcher to saw your
     turkeys in half—they're easier to freeze that way.

Seasonal Sales: Groceries

January	middle cuts of meat (standing ribs, steaks), possibly hams, party foods, frozen pizzas
February	any foods associated with Valentine's Day...on the fifteenth of the month
March	corned beef, maybe lamb
April/May	Mexican food products, eggs, ham, fish. Pork products may go down around Easter.
June/July	pop, potato chips, charcoal, paper plates, marshmallows, ketchup
October	candy (at the end of month)
November/ December	turkey, pumpkin, canned milk, sugars, cranberries, chocolate chips, nuts, cream cheese, baking ingredients

Seasonal Sales: Produce

January/ February	citrus fruits
March	citrus fruits, cabbage, rhubarb (In a colder season, produce prices may rise.)
April	asparagus, artichokes, potatoes (Warehouses clean out their storage to make room for the next crop.)
May	asparagus, strawberries
June	stone fruit, local onions, strawberries, variety melons
July	melons, California grapes, strawberries, corn, squash
August	best time for July items, cucumbers
September	apples (new crop), pears, corn, squash
October	apples (best time), squash, potatoes, yams
November	citrus season starts
December	citrus fruits, bananas (for baking), onions

They're also a more realistic size for family meals.

�֎ Seasonal beef slaughter is a bit higher in fall and early winter, which may spell relief for you. Meat prices, however, go up with demand for certain cuts.

Go to the Pro!

Watch out! Many growers make way for this year's new apple crop and potato crop by clearing the storage warehouses. This comes through as a sale around the time fall apple and potato harvest starts. Ask the produce manager, "Are these sale apples this year's crop?" Chance are 50–50 he'll say no.

Where to Shop for Food

Much of this chapter on food is based on my experience. For reference, Joe and I average less than $125 each month on food. (Our food budget does not include beverage or paper products.) How do we do it? Much depends on where we shop.

For one thing, I rarely go grocery shopping in the typical sense anymore. Once upon a time I studied the weekly grocery fliers, made a list, and zoomed into town. "Look at my bargains!" I would crow. What was I doing? For the most part, I was just buying for the sake of sales. I don't do that anymore.

I go into a regular, big-chain grocery store *maybe* once every couple of months when I am at home, and then only for a specific item not available elsewhere. Mainly, I shop four places: a warehouse store, a health food store, a dollar-type store (I kid you not), and farmer's markets. I also have a garden.

Throughout the years, I've managed to maintain a sensible stash of staples, predominantly including wheat-free pasta, rice, and beans. And what a variety of each I have! I build meals around these three staples, embellishing each dish with what I am using up, whether it is frozen hamburger or frozen

sliced peppers. Also, I am never without home-canned tomatoes. The bulk of our staples come from the warehouse store
and the health food store, and we visit each infrequently.

I can't tell you where to shop, but I can tell you where you
should *not* make a habit of shopping if you are budgeting your
food dollar: big name, big chain grocery stores, and gourmet
shops.

The mighty supermarket is probably where most people
shop. Unless your market is affiliated with a big-name discounter, you are paying a *lot* more for your groceries than you
need to. (One expert claims well over 30 percent more!) If you
shop in such a place, understand the tricks of the trade (under
"How to Shop for Food" in this section), and you will not be
swayed by merchandising gimmicks. In the meantime...

Most supermarkets expect a profit of 2 percent on goods.
However, "price sensitive" products cause the store to lose
some or all of that profit margin. Sometimes, a store may even
lose money on items due to price wars caused by competition
between markets and consumer demand. Price-sensitive items
commonly include mayonnaise, baby food, sugar, and tomato
or cream of mushroom soup.

Vendors compete with each other when selling their line of
food to supermarkets. That's one reason for seasonal price fluc-
tuations. Food manufacturers give "ad money" to stores. Some
markets use the ad money to offset losses by lowering prices
overall. These establishments will often have in-house sales
but do not publish weekly flyers for newspapers.

> *You have to decide if you're going to a supermarket*
> *for convenience or to save money because*
> *they're completely different things.*
>
> Clark Howard

As for the fancy shops, few people get a bigger kick out of toting home a nifty bag with the gourmet store's logo than I do. But is ego gratification worth paying more money than I'd pay *for the same thing* someplace else? Sometimes, yes, it is. Toting that bag home feels good. And I say go for it—*sometimes.* You can do that because you are so good with your food budget the rest of the time.

I buy in bulk at a warehouse and save around 26 percent of what I'd spend at the grocery store, *but I only buy the things we eat.* What is the sense in buying several jars of rosemary-scented capers—even if it is a good buy—if I will only use one jar in the next millennium?

I make quarterly visits to a favorite health food store to stock my pantry, and I will help you navigate your way through such a store in the next section. I buy our meat from a friend who raises grass-fed cows with no injections, I buy eggs from a local farmer, I usually make my own bread because it is fun, and I enjoy experimenting, and since we avoid wheat, I use alternative flours. I buy our olive oil from friends in California.

Note from me: In our house, we think of *good* olive oil as medicine.

Dollar-Type Stores?

Dollar-type stores are mystery tours. Joe and I like hard, dry-as-cardboard rye crackers, so I am able to buy several boxes at a time from such a store at a savings of around $1.70 per box. While there, I cruise the aisles to see if the store is carrying any organic overstock. I've also found screaming deals on canned beans and condiments at such stores.

50 Percent!

While places such as dollar-type stores can be gold mines for certain healthy foods, the vast majority of their food products fall into the category of "not so hot for your health."

Gardens

Our own garden keeps us in fresh produce throughout the growing season. We also have an established herb garden and a separate mint garden. Friends' gardens and the local farmers' market add to our abundance. I freeze what I can from the garden.

Try This!

Plant a small garden. Plant it in a big pot and put it on a window sill if you have no room. Lovingly tend your garden (organically, please). Experience the profound joy and connection to God's good earth when you harvest just what you need for dinner. No restaurant on earth can offer that kind of satisfaction!

Holy and Righteous Father, help me to become more careful with the bounty of Your good creation. May I not abuse what You have put in our care. And thank You, always, for Your providence! In Jesus' name. Amen.

50 Percent!

If circumstances allow, try to not buy groceries from a vendor who drives to your door.

What to Buy When Grocery Shopping

Let's understand each other up front: I am not against sugar or the right kind of fat. I am not against buying a bag of pretzels for the toddler to munch on or having a dark chocolate bar in the cupboard. (They can be healthy.) In my experience, eliminating these things from our diets is too extreme. They should be considered as they once were—treats. No one, however, especially children, should go within 50 feet of soda pop.

Soda not only packs a wallop with sugar (and don't get me started with diet drinks) but also has something called phosphoric acid (the stuff that makes the fizz that makes the sugar water taste so good) that sucks calcium out of our bones. (When you think of a soda straw, think of hollowed-out bones.) Hooray again for our son and daughter-in-law. I don't think either of our grandchildren has ever had soda. (Or maybe they just don't tell Grandma.)

Look—many of you reading this are trying. Hard. You want to feed your family a healthful diet, but your head is dizzy from the nonstop information that comes your way. I, myself, just fed you some information about pop.

If something harmful to your health is not in the house, you're not going to eat or drink it. I'm usually smart enough to know that if it's there, I will tell myself, *This one time. Tomorrow starts the new me.*

Reaching into a box of store-bought cookies or graham crackers is easy. And you should not feel chagrined about that. But you can just as easily make a huge batch of cookies without hydrogenated oils (that would be margarine) and freeze half, reach for a slice of cheese, enjoy a chunk of robust bread with some good butter and jam, or sample a piece of fruit. End of lecture.

Go to the Food Pro!

Jean Carper is a woman who writes extensively on food as medicine. I should have listed her in chapter 1 as one whom I hugely admire. In one of her books, *The Food Pharmacy,* she weighs in on sugar:

❀ Other than supplying calories and energy, sugar has no nutritional value.

❀ Eating sugar in excess can promote weight gain. (Many of those so-called low-fat products compensate for flavor with sugar.)

❁ In children, sugary food can replace nutritious food and promote cavities.

❁ Sugar can cause sharp spikes in insulin and blood glucose even though pure table sugar ranks below some foods, such as potatoes, carrots, and sticky rice.

So...What?

Every single solitary smart person I have read on the subject says the same thing about what to buy: the food along perimeters of the big markets. The thinking goes like this: Produce and dairy surround the processed stuff in the middle. This, of course, is not completely true. Good foods can be found down the aisles, but you get the idea.

If I were shopping in a standard grocery store, I surely would not buy my detergents and cleaning products, nor would I buy anything non-grocery. Those items are often less expensive elsewhere. For cleaning products I'd go to the warehouse store, buy bulk at the health food store, or go to an established janitor supply shop. For non-grocery, I'd probably go to a big discounter. The main thing you are buying at a big grocery is convenience. Sometimes you may need to opt for convenience. But once you get the hang of shopping and learn to retrain yourself, you will be able to gradually establish better habits—and save money in the mix.

So what about those health food stores? Aren't they expensive? What can you buy there? Plenty.

Tag Along!

Shopping in a health food store takes skill. Skill comes from practice, product knowledge, and knowing your prices. I will try to help you.

I learned the hard way. This is a true story: My first visit to a health food store was a *disaster*. I did four things wrong:

1. I didn't write on the bag whatever it was I bought, brought all kinds of weird-looking stuff home, didn't remember what it was, and ended up throwing most of it away.

2. I asked for a *pound* of bran. Do you have any idea how big a bag that is? Kept the entire population of Bigfork, Montana, regular for a month.

3. I spilled rice all over the floor (a veritable avalanche) because I couldn't figure how to work the self-serve mechanism.

4. I spent way too much money because I didn't know what I was doing.

So here are some tips from the school of hard knocks:

❀ In most cases, you are better off buying vitamin supplements at a warehouse store or at a major discounter.

❀ Boxed goods and canned goods are usually more expensive in a health food store. If you are concerned about being frugal, you probably don't buy too many convenience foods anyway because you probably cook from scratch as I do. Banish forever any goofy notions that cooking from scratch is too time consuming or hard.

❀ Organic fruits and veggies cost more. That is the simple, bottom line. In our house we buy organic when we can because we prefer the purity and taste and because we choose to support businesses that are more biblical in their treatment of land.

❀ Bottled *anything* costs money. Bottled anything in a health food store costs *more* money.

✺ Makeup, pet food, laundry (unless bulk), kitchen gadgets—forget it.

So what in the world does one buy?

✺ Health food stores cannot be beat for prices on herbs and spices. You can buy as little or as much as you like. (I buy my year's supply of bay leaves for around 50 cents.) I can keep my supply fresh (*very* important with herbs and spices), and I get a kick out of finding little jars for different spices.

✺ Rice. If you are fortunate to have a well-stocked and busy health food store nearby, the selection of bulk rice is often superior to that at a regular store. Most stores will give you the option to buy organic or not. Arborio, brown, white, long-grain, short-grain, and an assortment of other varieties are usually available.

✺ Beans and legumes. The selection is dazzling. And according to experts, we need to eat more beans. Yeah, yeah...the musical fruit. Go buy Beano.

✺ Flour. This is not usually a frugal item to buy in a health food store. Savings depend entirely upon what your preferences are. Certainly if you only need a cup of soy flour for a recipe, this is the place to go. Whole flours should be kept in a cool place to keep from going rancid.

✺ Bulk olive oil, soy, peanut butter, vinegar, molasses, honey, and regular oil. Most stores have a stash of jars and bottles that they will weigh before you fill, and they will deduct the jar weight at checkout.

✺ Oatmeal, hot cereals, bran, and seeds are usually a best buy here, but the warehouse might compete on oatmeal.

Note from me: Don't buy instant oats. They are a waste of your money because they are not so good for your body. Buy the real thing and cook your oats the old-fashioned way. Do this: Open one of those tiny bags of oat-flavored instant sugar and "natural flavors" (probably chemicals from a plant on the Jersey turnpike) and put the contents on a plate. Then put real, steel-cut oats in a pile next to that stuff. You make the call.

50 Percent!

❀ Yams are the kingpins of healthy veggies.

❀ Papaya is the Elvis Presley of fruits.

❀ Stick with color. The veggies that tend to be the most beneficial are the ones God wrapped in vibrant colors.

Go to the Pro!

❀ Buy inexpensive, tough cuts of meat and tenderize them with a marinade.

❀ Unless you want the bone to make soup, buy boneless ham. But buy whole-muscle, not one made by pressing ham scraps together. Some ham weight is nothing but added water.

Go to the Pet Food Pro!

My vet says that high-protein foods are not necessary for most dogs—and definitely not necessary for older ones! Food for older dogs should not contain excess protein, phosphorus, or sodium. It could hurt their kidneys.

50 Percent!

❀ Iceberg lettuce, the claims go, has no nutritional value and can be spendy at times. Buy less expensive leaf lettuce that is filled with vitamin A. To crisp: wash, dry, put in a baggie with a folded paper towel, and refrigerate.

❀ Healthy people, young or old, do not need vitamin drinks, which are a mixture of water, sugar, milk and soy protein, and a vitamin pill. Healthy people, young or old, need wholesome food. Eat a carrot (late in the day because of the glycemic index) and pocket the change.

How to Shop for Food

Any store you enter will have put serious thought into presenting their wares. Stores are not nonprofit organizations. They are in the business to make money. Nothing is wrong with that, and you should be happy to support your neighbors and friends by shopping at local stores. You should also know how.

The folks down at the mighty market, for instance, have invested megabucks to determine what lighting to use, what color to put on the walls, what music to play, how to present their products to make them irresistible, whether or not to carpet the floors, how to employ aromatherapy, and how to make themselves a one-stop shop so you keep coming back.

Nearly everyone has a favorite store. Arm yourself with skills so when you are in that favorite market, you won't be taken to the cleaners! Though I've shared some of these tips already, they bear repeating:

Super Strategies of Supermarkets

❀ The most expensive items are at eye level.

❀ The display at the end of the aisle is not always the best buy. (Grocers sometimes put nearly expired items here.)

❀ "Grouping" is displaying several different items in one place: chips with pop, salad dressings with produce, toppings with ice cream.

❀ Gourmet cheeses are displayed prominently. Surprise! You can usually buy the same cheese in the dairy case for less.

❀ The milk is in the back so you have to tramp through the entire store to get to it. I've noticed that "impulse" items like chips and cookies are suddenly appearing near dairy.

Go to the Milk Pro!

Experts say you are wasting your money if you buy milk in translucent plastic jugs. When exposed to fluorescent lighting, the milk oxidizes, develops a flat taste, and loses vitamin C.

50 Percent!

❀ Shop with cash. Leave your credit cards, your debit card, and your checkbook at home. Tell me how it went.

❀ After you fill your cart, pull over and take a long look. What can go back?

❀ Buy smaller if it's better, as in eggplant and other produce. Bigger fruits and veggies can be tougher, grainier, and even bitter. (By the way, buy eggplant that is heavy for its size.)

❀ Use a coupon only if you would normally buy the item, and try to use the coupon when the item is on sale.

❀ Watch ads for loss leaders. Know thy prices!

❀ Don't overbuy, even if something is on sale.

❀ Check the per-ounce price when comparing item prices. The bigger box used to be the better buy. That's not always the case anymore.

❀ Buy bulk—if the bulk per-ounce cost represents savings. Always consider your time and the cost of repackaging at home. I keep nearly all of my food in designated jars in our pantry. When I look on any shelf, my heart sings.

❀ Stay clear of convenience food: pre-seasoned chicken, stuffed pork chops, coleslaw mix, trimmed and sliced pineapple, even cut-up chicken. Consider the price against the *au natural* cost. Let's get real. Buy plain chicken, and when you get home, reach into the cupboard and grab some herbs and sprinkle. You need to use them anyway.

❀ Don't buy veggies in little bags with cheese sauce. Make your own with that chunk of cheese that is turning pink and green in your fridge. (Cut off the neon colors first.)

❀ Don't buy juice in cans or bottles—especially individual servings. If your children carry a lunch, go back to the old-fashioned thermos. (Cleaning the thermos is an excellent chore for kids after school.) If you buy juice, buy frozen or concentrate. (Incidentally, I read that you can refill an eight-ounce glass of water up to 15,000 times for the same cost as a six-pack of pop.)

❀ Buy industrial-sized cans of certain foods. Can you freeze some of the product in smaller containers?

❀ Check a sale item against the generic or store brand.

❀ Stock up on meat when it's on sale if you have a freezer. And then *use* it.

❀ Try not to buy lunchmeat at the deli. Buy a precooked ham or turkey ham and ask the meat department to slice it to your liking. Be certain the slicing doesn't cost extra.

❀ At times, meat and cheese "ends" are less expensive. If you insist on buying deli, ask about this.

❀ Regard all meat as expensive.

❀ Try chicken thighs as a tasty alternative to boneless breasts. (Chicken is one of the foods we are adamant about eating organic. It is expensive for us, so chicken is a treat.)

❀ Never buy a dairy product without checking its expiration date. The package with the longest shelf life is usually found toward the back of the display.

❀ Shredded or sliced cheese costs more. Ask the meat department if they will slice the brick of cheese you bought on sale. And good grief, already—use your arm muscles. Slightly freeze the cheese and shred it yourself.

❀ Do not buy yogurt in individual containers unless you have first checked that the price per ounce is cheaper or unless you only need a little. Buy the quart size. Buy plain and flavor it yourself.

Try This!

Add confectionery sugar and a bit of orange, almond, or vanilla flavoring to a cup of plain yogurt.

Stopwatch!

Do you know when you are most vulnerable in grocery stores? When you grab your cart and head into the store. Keep your shopping time short. The longer you are in there, the bigger your bill. Duh.

Try This!

Ever buy a five-pound sack of spuds? Or apples? Or oranges? Next time you do, take three sacks to the hanging scale and weigh each. Odds are you'll find a five-pound sack that weighs closer to six pounds.

Food, The Keeping of

Proper storage of food is a huge part of saving money. Why spend judiciously if you lose your savings through neglect, rot, or decay? This is such an important issue with me that I have provided a Produce Respiration Table in two of my books, *Living Well on One Income* and *1001 Bright Ideas to Stretch Your Dollars.* I do this because very few of us have learned how to properly store produce—not to mention meats, cheeses, coffee beans, flours, rice...and on and on.

Waste Not!

Make a conscious effort to never let produce turn into green goop in your fridge again. This is an important principle: *Buy only what you need* when you buy produce. Some stores will actually break bunches of produce and sell you a lesser amount. Let's say you only need a stalk of celery, and that celery (or parsley or cilantro or lettuce) *always* goes bad in your fridge. Purchase wisely. If it turns to rot, your money (and God's providence) went into the trash.

50 Percent!

❀ Plastic bags are indispensable for storing certain produce, but they can trap moisture. Too much moisture is not good, so poke a few "breather" holes in the bag. Especially for carrots—they hate to be "trapped."

❀ Carrots stored near apples will become bitter.

❀ Put folded newspaper on the bottom of your crisper.

❀ Do *not* store potatoes in the fridge (same with avocados). Store them in a dark, dry place. Cold converts potato starch to sugar, which makes black blotches inside your spuds. Also, do not store potatoes with onions, since each gives off gas that affects the other. (Maybe we should give them some Beano...)

❀ Store bananas, stone fruit, and tomatoes at room temperature unless they are fully mature, when they can be refrigerated. Even bananas! The skin will turn black, but they will last longer.

❀ Keep plastic produce bags to double up and use as "suitcases" for freezer-wrapped goods.

❀ Use or freeze leftovers promptly. Just because Missy didn't finish her milk doesn't mean the cat gets it. Cover it and put it in the fridge for her next thirst attack. She'll get the message.

❀ Don't keep meat in the freezer too long. Meat begins to lose nutritional value after six months—hamburger after three months.

❀ Freeze pieces of meat individually on a tray when processing family packs. Once the meat is frozen solid, store the pieces in larger freezer bags.

❀ Breads stale quickly in cold temperatures. Most bread should be kept out of the refrigerator.

❀ Pasta can lose up to 20 percent of its riboflavin if stored in plastic and up to 80 percent if stored in decorative glass containers.

❀ Cut the leaves off root veggies (carrots, radish, and beets) before storing, and you'll get more vitamins.

Save those greens! Some people like the taste of radish greens in their salads. Beet greens are filled with good stuff for you—hide them in soup or chop and add to stir-fry.

Go to the Coffee Pro!

Do not store coffee in the fridge. Keep extra beans in the freezer, and have a week's supply or so on hand in an airtight container in a cupboard. All the coffee snobs claim this. Honest. (I get fitful mail on this one.)

Tag Along!

All of a sudden, I found myself with way more bread than we could possibly eat. What to do? Simple. I sliced the bread and put each slice in a sandwich bag, and then I put all the bagged bread into a bigger ziplock freezer bag. All I had to do was take out the slices I needed. *And I didn't make more bread until the stuff in the freezer was gone.* Don't roll your eyes—it took about one minute, two at the most.

Try This!

Ever need green or red bell peppers for a recipe in the middle of winter? Do you stir-fry often? Red peppers, in particular, can be costly. (Red peppers are green peppers, but older.) Bell peppers are as easy as 1-2-3 to freeze. Buy them when they are in season and inexpensive, cut them into slices or chunks (to the compost with the insides!), plop them in the freezer bag, get out as much air as possible, and toss in the freezer.

Food, The Eating of

Here is where I shine! Not a gourmet cook by a long shot, I just take whatever is on hand and turn it into a meal. Most of the time my meals start from scratch—sometimes scratching my noggin while I'm looking at the cupboard and thinking, *hmm...*

Homemade or Store-Bought?

Even if you are zealous about losing weight and saving money, you would be unrealistic to expect to eliminate all convenience from life. A product or machine may clear your time for more important purposes. And though you choose what you put into a homemade recipe (to make it healthy and lo-cal), homemade is not always thrifty. Because homemade substitutes can save money, however, I have included a list of substitutions in the appendix.

Some basic tips for food preparation may help you:

❀ Read recipes ahead of time. Twice. Then think them through.

❀ Measure—unless you are a grandmother.

❀ Use meat as an ingredient, not as the main event.

❀ People feast with their eyes—presentation is everything! As a matter of fact, it's about 70 percent of the appeal of the meal.

❀ Make a small piece of meat look big by serving it on something: a bed of lettuce, rice, or a piece of bread.

❀ Ever end up with leftover snacks in the bottom of a big bowl? As the supply dwindles, transfer what's left to smaller and smaller bowls. It's more appealing that way.

❀ Don't waste crushed tortilla chips or potato chips—stir them into scrambled eggs. Or heat pinto beans and cheese and plop the mixture on top of crushed chips. Or crush more to use as breading.

❀ One teabag in a pot of water is more than enough to brew tea. Just steep it longer.

❀ Freeze the juice from canned fruit and plop it in a blender with milk. Whir away.

Go to the Vitamin Pro!

Experts claim taking your vitamins on an empty stomach is a waste of money. If you take them in the morning, take them after breakfast. And if you take fat-soluble vitamins like A or E, take them after you've had a full meal—especially one with some fat in it.

50 Percent!

❀ Eat 50 percent slower.

❀ Use smaller bowls, plates, glasses, mugs, and cups. Eat soup with a teaspoon.

❀ Eat 50 percent smaller servings of foods that tend to add to your waistline.

❀ Eat 50 percent larger servings of such vegetables as celery, radish, greens, cucumbers, tomatoes, cabbage, onions, garlic, string beans, and peppers.

❀ Chew 50 percent longer before you swallow.

❀ Try not to eat on the run.

❀ Drink 50 percent more water if you need more water consumption, but be sure you are not throwing off your electrolyte balance. Water is utterly vital to our health and most of us don't drink enough. So...

Try This!

Have you ever considered how much money you would save if you substituted water half the time you reach for a beverage? Nothing could be better for you. Water regulates body temperature, carries nutrients and oxygen to cells, and removes wastes. It also cushions joints and helps protect organs and tissues. And while I'm at it, why don't we give our young children water anymore? What's up with that?

❉ Take a water break instead of a coffee break.

❉ Drink water before meals or snacks.

❉ Take water along when traveling.

❉ Treated water from the tap can harm the mineral balance in your body, especially iodine. A good water filter on the tap is a *must* for good health.

Pink Giraffe

Good. I have your attention again. So listen some more:

In addition to my concern about the number of diabetics escalating, I believe we have a new concern on the horizon: celiac disease. Yeah, yeah...I know. We have some new scare every few years. (Maybe we just know more.) I often read about people who are allergic to the gluten in wheat and people who are allergic to *all* gluten. Sometimes failure to thrive, failure to lose weight, and failure to feel good has to do with a bona fide food allergy. Check with your doc...but I warn you: Many doctors pooh-pooh this notion. Could it be that many people feel good and lose weight on the low-carb regimens because they have proscribed wheat products from their diets? Just a thought.

50 Percent!

❀ Nuts are expensive (but healthy!) Use half the nuts needed in a recipe:

1. Simply use fewer nuts. Chop them well.
2. Use shelled, unsalted sunflower seeds.
3. Toast real oatmeal and add it to your to batter.
4. Use a Grape-Nuts type cereal.

❀ Too much salt in your soup? Add a couple of slices of raw potato and simmer awhile. Too much pepper? Add butter. Too sweet? Add salt.

Stopwatch!

Cut your cooking time in half!

❀ Make enough dinner to fill lunch pails the next day. Put leftovers in small Tupperware. In the morning, grab the container, a piece of fruit, a jug of water, and go on your merry way.

❀ Try to cook twice as much soup, spaghetti sauce, chili, or stew as you need. Freeze half. *And use what you freeze* (same year, please).

Quick Potato Salad: Cook new red potatoes, don't skin. Cut into small chunks. Chop anything else you want: peppers, onion, celery, carrot, and more. Throw it all in a bowl. Pour on Italian dressing. Put in fridge for a while. Add more dressing if it dries out too much. The end.

Here's a neat trick for freezing hamburger: Put it into a plastic freezer bag, smush it down so that it covers the inside of the entire bag (thereby pushing out air), and seal the bag. Cooking said burger is easy too, because you can simply make little meat patties rather than meatballs. (Just cut the bag off the meat when you take it from the freezer.)

Try This!

❊ What is getting long in the tooth in your fridge? Build your next meal around it. If you can't, then freeze it if you can. Don't let it go to waste. Let me give you an example: Suppose you have two fresh apples. (Well, they *were* fresh two weeks ago!) Rather than open a jar of applesauce for dinner, use what you have. Peel, core, and cube the apples, and cook them with a bit of water. Serve "cubed applesauce" with walnuts and honey and a little cinnamon. When you no longer have fresh stuff on hand, *then* you open the applesauce.

❊ Yams are loaded with beta-carotenes. Cut them into thinish wedges, coat with olive oil, sprinkle with salt, and bake on a cookie sheet at 400 degrees till crisp on the outside and soft on the inside. Bet you can't eat just one. Incidentally, in the long run, a good quality toaster oven may cost less than heating your full-size oven.

❊ Shred fresh-peeled potatoes and pack them into a hot waffle-iron coated with non-stick spray. Waffle hash browns!

❊ Discover your creative genius! Make your usual meat-loaf concoction. Roll it out about one-inch thick on waxed paper. Make a rectangle. Then put on whatever your heart desires: pre-cooked veggies, mashed potato, sliced cheese, tomatoes...look in the fridge and find something that needs using. Now, use the waxed paper to help you to roll your creation jelly-roll style. Pinch the ends closed. Transfer to baking pan and bake uncovered at 350 degrees about 1 1/4 hours. Cut into slices. Serve with waffle hash browns.

50 Percent!

Steakout! Have you ever provided a big steak for each guest at a cookout? You splurged to begin with, only to watch the spaniel devour the leftovers from each plate. Our rule is to buy half as many steaks as you have guests, cook them (steaks, not guests), cut each steak into three pieces, plop the pieces on a platter, and enjoy the leftovers at midnight. Give the dog a bone.

Try This (for the Small Fry)!

Here is a fun project for you and the kids: S-t-r-e-t-c-h that food! Get three potatoes.

❀ Bake one (stab it with fork a few times and microwave for six to eight minutes.)

❀ Cut one into quarters and steam (you can do this in a microwave too.)

❀ Cut one into small cubes, steam it, and top with butter.

Which potato served more people?

50 Percent!

Unless you are buying your eggs from a local farmer or from an honest-to-goodness, no-fooling supplier whose chickens *do* roam and scratch, don't waste your money on "free range" claims these days. This marketing gimmick usually means the chickens can actually *move* in their crates.

Eggs are very healthy for you. And they are inexpensive. If you have never had a real egg—the kind that comes from a chicken that eats a healthy diet and does get to scratch around, you are in for a surprise. The taste, quality, and color is outstanding.

Ten Things to Do with Four Things

For a bit of whimsy, I have selected four foods and have concocted ten things to do with each. I hope you enjoy!

Eggs

1. Hard boil. Mark shells with "HB" and put in a bowl in the fridge. *Do not leave at room temperature.* Makes a terrific snack.

2. Hard boil for egg salad. Use nonfat plain yogurt instead of mayo. Include chopped celery. Sprinkle with paprika.

3. Make a frittata! (A whattata?) Beat five or so eggs (leave out the yolk from three if you are a fat watcher) and put them in a greased frying pan. Sprinkle top with anything. We have used thin apple slices and cinnamon, grated cheese, minced onion, leftover veggies, and leftover meat pieces. Cover with lid until it all cooks.

4. Make an omelet. Same as above, but flip over.

5. See the appendix for a recipe for Dead Cheese Pie.

6. Beat an egg or two and add slowly to hot chicken broth.

7. Hard boil, cut in half. Mash the yolk together with seasoning, chopped pickles, or chopped olives. Spoon mixtures into hollowed egg halves, or fill celery stalks.

8. Toast a fat piece of bread. Cut a round circle out of its center. Put on a hot griddle. Plop an egg inside and cook. I think this is called Toad in the Hole.

9. Garnish a salad and add protein to your meal. Simply cut hard-boiled eggs into slices.

10. Scramble with home fries for a terrific meal. Or serve over easy with waffle hash browns.

Apples

1. Eat as they are. Wash with mild detergent and water first. Trust me.

2. Cut into slices, spread peanut butter or cream cheese on each slice, and drizzle with wheat germ.

3. Core the apples and fill the holes with any combination of the following: dab of butter, chopped nuts, raisins, maple syrup, honey, brown sugar, white sugar, or cinnamon candies. Bake in 350-degree oven till apples are soft. You can do this in the microwave too.

4. Put sliced apples into the bottom of a baking pan, sprinkle some sugar on top, let sit a good half hour. Next, plop on a "crisp" topping (check your cookbook). Bake one-half hour at 350 degrees.

5. Peel, core, slice, cook. Make applesauce. No need to add sweetener to most apples.

6. Shred into pancake batter. Oh boy, this is good!

7. Put thin slices on top of omelet and sprinkle with a bit of sugar and cinnamon.

8. Heat butter in a frying pan, add cored, peeled, and sliced apples, and sauté till apples get awesome brown spots from the frying. Then sprinkle with powdered cardamom. This is an amazing recipe.

9. Shred into salads.

10. Shred onto a slice of bread or English muffin, top with cheese, and heat till cheese melts.

Bananas

1. Eat as they are.

2. Freeze as is, right in the peel (especially when it's getting long in the tooth) to use later for baking. Better yet, peel it, stick it in a baggie, and mash it to get rid of air before freezing.

3. Dip pieces in chocolate. Create a fondue for the kids. Or dip the entire banana in chocolate and freeze.

4. A favorite! Cut in pieces, smear with peanut butter, and roll in wheat germ.

5. Frozen, mushy, or fresh: Put in blender with milk and a little orange juice, and sweeten if you like. Whir. (Add vanilla and powdered milk and ice cubes for a tasty treat.)

6. Make a salad! Add orange pieces, grapes, some coconut, and drizzle with orange juice.

7. Make a banana split! (I'm on my way over.)

8. Add to cookie mix.

9. Put chunks in pancakes.

10. Make banana bread.

Ten Things for the Small Fry: Saltine Crackers

1. Eat as they are.

2. Spread with soft butter. I ate *thousands* when I was a kid.

3. Make mini peanut butter and jelly sandwiches. Caution! Be sure your peanut butter is very soft before you spread. Make any kind of mini, open-faced sandwiches. Call them *crackerwiches*.

4. Polish goulash: This is going to sound gross, but it is an old family favorite. I think my grandmother invented this during the Depression. Crumble saltines in a cereal bowl, add milk and sugar. Eat away. I know it sounds yucky, but it is really good! (Caveat: I think sauerkraut is really good too.)

5. Crumble and put in bottom of soup bowl, pour soup on top. Or crumble on top of soup or stew. Also, consider using crushed crackers to thicken stew.

6. Make pie crust for quiche. Crush in blender, add couple tablespoons of melted butter, mix. Pat in pie tin.

7. Crush in blender and use as bread crumbs.

8. Crumble, soften with a little milk, and add to meat loaf or hamburgers.

9. Crumble into salad at last minute. You don't want them to get soggy.

10. Donate to food bank. First, have the kids copy these Ten Things to attach to each box.

50 Percent!

Skim milk and nonfat milk are pretty much the same except skim has a little more body because nonfat milk solids are added.

Try This!

To me, meals are the nucleus of family life. We should invest maximum effort into making this time special to the family. They will learn to look forward to it, and it will become a symbol of the ultimate marriage feast that we long for as children of God.

❀ Do everything in your power to come together as a family for meals.

❀ Make meals a time to stop, slow down, and commune with each other, to cherish each other, and to celebrate each other.

❀ Never eat without prayer.

❀ Make your table rumba (when you are up to the task).

❀ Teach your children manners, but don't go over the top. Let laughter ring at your table.

❀ Don't turn your meal into the Grand Inquisition. If someone chooses to share events of the day, that's terrific.

❀ Delegate one evening as Soup Night. We do this on Monday, giving our systems a little rest from heavier digestive duties.

❀ Delegate one night as International Night. Ask the children to decorate: Draw and color the flag of the country, learn some customs, and learn where the country is.

❀ Once in a while, honor a specific family member at dinner with a special plate, a gift, or a break from evening chores.

❀ In our family, whoever cooks usually doesn't clean up.

❀ Bring back the Sunday table!

Give us this day our daily bread...

Polish: *Chleba nashego powsiedniego daj nam dzisiaj.*

French: *Donne-nous notre pain quotidien.*

My ethnic background is Polish and French. What's yours?

Eating Out

You may have caused me to shrink in horror at my sinful nature, Cynthia, or to feel shame for the lack of the fruit of the Spirit in my life. You may have encouraged me to get a grip, and to deconstruct my thinking to live a more content life. But you're going too far if you go after the one luxury I have in life. Go after my closets, go after my veggie bin, even go after my lattes, but leave my French fries alone!

Sorry.

Want to save money? Stay home and cook. Zip by the arches, forgo the tacos, and turn your car toward home. I know it's not so easy. You've got all those errands and cooking would just be too stressful, right?

So make a sandwich. Who says dinner has to be a hot meal?

First Rule for Saving Money When Eating Out: Don't

Am I saying you should never go to a restaurant? Of course not. Rather, I'm suggesting you return to a previous time when a restaurant visit was a treat or special occasion. Get out of the habit of using the drive-through for the sake of convenience. Some studies show that we spend up to 40 percent of our food dollar on eating out. That is a big chunk of moola. And be honest—doesn't it get *old* after a while?

Connect the dots. Before you spend your shekels on restaurant food, think about what you could buy at the grocer's. How about a roast you wouldn't ordinarily buy, or a big turkey? Seven billion pounds of rice? A gazillion grapes? And what about the pounds you pack on your waistline from the food you pack in your mouth when you eat at a restaurant? If you quit going out half the time, you would be way ahead of the game. Financially, maybe 20 percent ahead.

But what if you're really not in the mood to make a meal? And suppose you are in the mood for, you know, God's gift to mankind: *pizza!* Why not waltz over to your freezer and pull out a good quality frozen pizza you purchased at the warehouse store? Should you never order a pizza? Don't be silly. Just remember that you have other options.

How Not to Go to a Restaurant

If your intent is to be healthier and more frugal, forgo the fast food, go home, and prepare your meal. Notice I didn't say "cook." So what can you do in a hurry?

❀ Serve a selection of quality cold cereal tonight. Present the cereals in an assortment of pretty bowls. Add sliced banana. Sounds like a good meal to me: milk, grain, and fruit.

❀ Make yogurt sundaes. If you have tall, clear glasses, layer cut fruit with flavored yogurt. Top with coconut, chopped nuts, or colored sprinkles left over from holiday cookie baking.

❀ Make peanut butter and jelly sandwiches. Or jelly and cream cheese sandwiches. Or peanut butter and banana, or cream cheese and cucumbers, or lettuce and tomato, or onions and liverwurst (just kidding on that last one).

❀ Take every single jar of pickles, olives, and condiments from the fridge. Open a can or two of tuna. Grab a little of each veggie that you can serve raw. Check to see if you have any leftover cheese. Drain a can of garbanzo beans. Arrange everything on a big platter and serve with bread.

❀ Make banana splits. The kids will think you've lost your mind (but secretly they will think, *waaay cool!*). If you use fresh, real fruit, real whipped cream, and walnuts, this is not such a horrible meal as it sounds.

50 Percent!

❀ Go to a fancy restaurant for dessert and coffee. Call ahead to see if this is okay, and don't go during their busy hours. Get all dressed up.

❀ Ask if you can split a plate. Wonder Man and I do this all the time.

❀ Do not buy appetizers unless the appetizer will be your meal.

❀ Use coupons. Some merchant groups offer coupon books (for a fee) that give many two-for-one deals at restaurants. Careful—some of the coupons have weird conditions. *"Coupon good on the night of a full moon on the second Thursday of the week if you were born in a leap year at 6:01 A.M, and if you are completely dressed in orange. Otherwise, full price, Toots."*

❀ Avoid dinner altogether. Go to a nice place for breakfast or lunch. Some places let you purchase from the lunch menu in the evening.

❀ All beverages in restaurants are expensive. Ask for water with a wedge of lemon.

❀ Try to not buy dessert unless that is what you went for.

❀ Monday night's fish special is Friday's fish delivery. (One chef I read said to never eat swordfish. Don't ask.)

Try This (for the Small Fry)!

How much school lunch money do you dole out every day? Multiply that amount by five days, then by four weeks, and you now know how much you spend each month. After the shock wears off, take my advice:

❀ Don't completely deny your children the fun of getting school lunch. Allow one or two days each week for them to purchase lunch. They will know when pizza is on the menu!

❀ Make the lunch you send to school fun and interesting. Put stickers on lunch sacks or on the baggie holding the sandwich. Include notes (not too mushy or corny) or funny jokes inside the lunch box. Include a forbidden fruit like candy from time to time.

❀ Find something to use as a surprise gift sack. Every once in a while, put something in the sack—a coin, a promise to do something that evening, a nifty new pencil or eraser. Stuff the sack in your child's lunch. Call it a Sack Attack.

❀ Don't let Madison Avenue influence your kids! Those wretched little lunch packages are not only expensive but also loaded with bad fats and salt. Fake food, if you ask me.

❀ Children will usually eat food they took part in preparing.

❀ Put ice cream in a wide-mouth thermos and freeze overnight. It is supposed to be perfect by lunch time. If it melts too much, send a straw and call it a shake.

50 Percent!

Worried about your weight when eating out? Don't forget ownership! Tell your server that you are watching your health.

❀ Ask for substitutions. Don't ask a lone, harried server to do this when the place is packed and people waiting for a table are stacked like cordwood. Use common sense. Be polite. The answer may be no.

❋ Ask if you can purchase a half serving.

❋ Scout out the buffet. It may have a bonanza of fresh veggies for you.

❋ Stay clear of sauces that cover the taste of the real food.

❋ Go to a place that serves healthy foods.

❋ Ask for real butter, real maple syrup, and filtered water (*Careful!* The cost of fancy bottled water in a restaurant is out of sight! Some restaurants have started a new gimmick. They have the bottle on the table when you are seated. Ask what it costs.) Also ask for your veggies slightly steamed, no bread unless it is hearty, real olive oil and Balsamic vinegar for your salad, and that on the side.

The Tale of a Bad Day

(This women's tale is identical to the mother who works outside the home. It picks up where this stay-at-home mom begins to think about her day.)

You begin to think about the day: Drive Missy and Junior to school and preschool, drop off dry cleaning and fight with the clerk about the stain in your favorite dress, search for missing Disney DVD, meet with playgroup, attend meeting at preschool with a healthy snack (whatever that means anymore. Just how many mini-carrots can kids take?), call the vet to find out if Barky needs her stomach pumped from all those shells, search for your marriage manual before you do something evil to your husband's shirts, and oh yes—do your stretching exercise, drink more water, walk vigorously around the block with Precious, do your Sunday school lesson, and freak out about finances.

Once again you feel guilty for your decision to stay at home, but your intent to be there for everyone 24/7 is noble. It *is* better for the children, and why should you feel guilty that you are not contributing financially? You do everything in your power to scrimp and conserve and save money. But how you miss the chance to use your education and to make a difference on a broader scale.

You touch your long, wet hair. Your mind drifts to one of those makeover shows you saw on TV. (Now you feel guilty about *that* too—*watching TV* instead of, like, retiling the bathroom floor? What's the matter with you?) You let out a big sigh. You've really let yourself go since you've been home all the time. I mean, why get out of your sweats for the kids? You are not complaining. But that's your whole world anyway...kids...

To be continued...

10
House Stuff

She looks well to the ways of her household.

PROVERBS 31:27 KJV

I have always admired the Proverbs 31 woman. That lady is one class act. Strong, resourceful, good in business, terrific with a sewing machine, unbeatable in the kitchen, cheerful. Every time I read Proverbs 31, I respect her more—especially when I remember this is God speaking. She is His kind of gal. Cool. No Donna Reed there. This woman is interactive with her world. Not in high heels, but standing with both feet on the ground, hands on hips, a glint in her eye, and self-assurance that won't quit. No Xena the Warrior Princess either. She is filled with grace, charm, kindness, and magnetism that makes me want to be like her. I wish I were a Proverbs 31 woman.

What about you? The Proverbs 31 woman looks well to the ways of her household. Do you sometimes look *away* from your harried household? Regardless of your resolve, does the care of your house get away from you?

Home, The Caring of

Once upon a time, a woman who stayed home and cared for her house and children had a lovely routine. Monday was wash day, Tuesday was ironing day, and on and on. Now, whether

177

you stay at home or work outside the home, you struggle to keep up in this complicated and stressed-out society. You are dulled from constant stimulation and tired from constant vigilance. Who is trying to rip you off, how are the kids getting educated, what are the kids being educated? All this and dust? Too much. Once upon a time, life was...different.

If we fast-forward from Babci and her cronies milling around the stew pot, we bump into all sorts of things, including many, many single-parent families. Single parent or not, you are busily commuting to your job, ferrying the kids to endless activities, trying to maintain sound nutrition, recharging your batteries so you can stay awake past 8:00 P.M.—while dust accumulates on the TV screen, layers of exploded food build in the microwave, and thick soap scum coats the shower. Housekeeping is a big job!

Organize!

Want to cut your work by up to 50 percent? Get rid of your clutter. Appraise your home now: How much time do you spend shuffling stuff around, picking through laundry baskets to find clothes, standing on a kitchen chair to dig through your spice cupboard to find the basil, ducking when you reach for a coffee mug for fear of getting bonked, or digging through your purse again to find your kid's library card...?

Organization will save you time, money, and tons of stress. In turn, you won't reach for the potato chips, which will, in turn help a little toward staying healthy and slim. The one thing in my life that keeps me running like a finely tuned engine is organization. Some of you may think that you just aren't the type to stay organized. Oh, please. Unless you are ADHD, organization is a skill, not a genetic trait. Skills can be learned and practiced until they are second nature. I'm going to teach you some of those skills now by example.

Tag Along!

It's morning. I pad down the long hall to our big kitchen and flip a light switch. I'm greeted by hundreds of tiny white lights that adorn swags of bare branches over tall windows and are intertwined with year-round artificial pine garland atop our cupboards. The twinkle lights put me in a terrific mood, even on a dreary day. Sweet, gentle music plays in the background. I begin my morning routine: Heat water for tea, empty the dishwasher, think about the day's meals...

Tea water takes time, so I do that first, putting the kettle on a burner that matches its size. I empty the dishwasher while the water heats. Everything that comes out of the dishwasher has its place in the kitchen. Thick, white coffee mugs go into a cupboard to join others—just enough for us and some company. I don't stack any mugs atop one another since I've learned that we can only use so many. (Surplus mugs went the way of the yard sale a long time ago.) Same with drinking glasses. We have neat rows of different-sized glasses. Nothing fancy, all dollar-store-type stuff, but all in place.

Cooking utensils and wooden spoons go into their own container near the stove. Pots and their lids go on sliding shelves. Dishes and bowls have homes on shelves where they are accessible and not crowded.

Water boiling, I take an old teapot from our tea cupboard and go through the pleasant ritual of deciding which tea to brew. Our teas are in an assortment of old tea tins, all marked and easily available.

I reach into the appliance garage on our counter and pull our Vita-Mix toward me. (I don't like appliances displayed on counters.) By now I've thought about the day's meals—not *how* I will prepare food, but *what* I will prepare. (Does anything need using? Does anything need defrosting?) I reach into the fridge for ingredients for our morning health shake and whir away.

On automatic pilot, everything happens in less than five minutes. No hassle, cramming, jamming, stuffing, ducking, or operating by the seat of my pants.

Why am I telling you this? You are most likely a slave to your stuff. Get rid of half of it, and you will free enough time and space to become organized. And then practice. Pretty soon you'll be on automatic pilot too.

Try This!

Clean out and organize a few things for a quick boost:

❀ your wallet

❀ your purse

❀ your briefcase

❀ your silverware drawer

❀ Advanced organization: Put on your gloves and inventory your freezer.

Tag Along—Long Ago!

You already know I'm old-fashioned about children. But have you ever considered how much extra work you make for yourself by letting them have the run of the house? When our son was young, I used a playpen. Not a cage; a playpen. (What happened to these things, anyway?) Of *course* he had freedom to wander around the house and play. But when *I* needed to wander around and get something accomplished, when I needed to clean an area, when I needed some freedom from the nonstop attention to his every move, in he went. He was accustomed to his playpen and liked it. I saw to it that he wasn't alone in that thing or unable to watch *my* every move.

Think Small and Think Short-Term

At times I've thought cleaning the house was a waste of time. After all, it will just get dirty again. But what is the alternative? Living in a landfill? That's sort of like saying you won't shovel snow because spring is coming. Two months from now. Living in a cleanish, somewhat ordered house simply makes life easier. Organization brings order and routine that help you weather impossibly demanding times because you *are* on automatic pilot. If you look at the big picture, however, you can be discouraged, especially if your entire home looks like "who did it and ran." Take it slowly. Start with that wallet. Or the silverware drawer. (And while you're at it, use those neat serving spoons in an exotic rice dish tonight.)

Home tending involves many and varied skills, and it is an art. Hundreds of tips are available to help make the care of your castle easier. I've selected several which I feel are most valuable.

Go to the Appliance Pro!

❀ Cheap detergents have an abundance of filler (such as salt, the cheapest part of laundry detergent, which softens water). This gives you less cleaning power.

❀ Vacuum under your refrigerator regularly. This is where you will find the fan and the condenser. It is also where you will find pet hairs and dust balls and Legos.

❀ Clean your hot water heater every year. This is important.

❀ Change your vacuum cleaner bags regularly! This is beyond important.

❀ Vacuum often; your carpet will last much longer. (Dirt acts like little scissors on fibers.) Vacuum in two different directions.

182 © Ditch the Diet and the Budget

❀ Use carpet runners and entrance mats. Go shoeless inside the home.

❀ Use a professional squeegee when washing windows. For an effective window washing solution, try water. If this sounds squirrelly to you, add one drop of dish detergent to one quart of water. (I suppose you could add a smidgen of blue food coloring, but why?)

50 Percent!

One of the first places to eliminate clutter is under your kitchen sink. Cut your cleaning costs by 50 percent by cleaning under there and using all your cleaning products before you buy another one.

Go to the Pro!

❀ Some home improvements pay for themselves if you ever sell: updating plumbing, electrical or heating, fixing driveway cracks, painting the inside (keep colors neutral!), updating kitchen or bath, and keeping a well-manicured, low-care lawn.

❀ Some home improvements do not pay for themselves: swimming pools, hot tubs, fireplaces, expensive windows, marble floors, expensive fixtures, costly decks, or room additions.

❀ For a low-cost way to enhance the value of your home, consider a flower garden.

50 Percent!

❀ Rather than purchase that rototiller, carpet cleaner, power saw, or post-hole digger, rent or borrow, unless the purchase is absolutely justified. But if you borrow, return it in better condition than when you received it.

❀ Borrow a friend's small appliance (such as a pasta maker), use it at home, and determine if using and cleaning the contraption is worth its purchase. Lots of "must have" small appliances end up taking valuable space in the kitchen and sit unused. If you must have a small appliance, but use it infrequently, store it in an out-of-the-way spot to create more usable kitchen space.

Stopwatch!

Alrighty then. Here's the typical scenario:

We dry the laundry. We schlep the laundry to the TV room, even if it's on another floor, to begin the dreaded folding, during which time the kids come along and make a mess of everything we folded. We eventually schlep the laundry to designated dressers and closets, usually on another floor. This is a no-brainer:

Bring the dried load to the bedroom where most clothes belong and plop it on the bed. Separate clothes by person and then by type of clothing.

Let's say you have a pile of men's undershirts. Fold and place them immediately in man's dresser. Use a little swivel motion in your hips. Movement is health.

Ten Home-Tending Tidbits

1. A handful of salt in a quart of water should remove perspiration stains.

2. Make cut flowers last by trimming the stems every few days. And change that smelly water!

3. A fire burns better on top of a bed of ash.

4. Use Vaseline on a squeaky door.

5. Try Vaseline or mayonaise on a white ring mark on a wooden table. Put it on at night and wipe it off in the morning.

6. Rub cornmeal into a grease spot on the couch, let it sit a couple of hours, and then vacuum.

7. Cover the arms of upholstered furniture.

8. Remove rust from tools by making a paste of 2 tablespoons salt and 1 teaspoon lemon juice. Rub away.

9. Check your forced-air furnace filters and replace them if they're dirty.

10. The laundry room is a prime place for house fires. Lint clogs trap heat, and lint acts like dry tinder on a fire. Lots of junk is stored in the laundry room too.

Go to the Landscape Pro!

❀ Have a stressed-out tree? Pour milk on the roots. Trees love calcium.

❀ You can find better buys on trees and perennials in the fall because nurseries don't want to overwinter their stock.

❀ Buy healthy plants in the fall. In the spring, energy goes to making buds; in the fall, energy goes to sinking roots.

❀ Not a good idea to plant a tree in the heat of summer.

❀ Fertilize your lawn every fall.

Home, The Cutifying of

Radio host: So where do you get decorations for your house, Cynthia? (He expects me to recommend my favorite craft store.)

Me: Outside.

Radio host: ...(dead silence.)

Your personality and character spill into your living space. The building that was once an assortment of rooms where you placed beds and tables and desks and toy chests takes on a character that reflects your very spirit. My house? I'd like to think of it as one big smile, a sanctuary for man or beast, with doors flung open for all to enter. The sound of a wooden screen door slamming sends my heart soaring to the very hem of heaven! Noise around our table? Too wonderful for me to bear! Curtains drawn wide on our many tall windows so that sun-shine, clouds, snow, and rain seem to pour right onto our laps? Divine!

Tag Along!

Here are some of my "outside" seasonal decorations:

Winter: I am fortunate to have an unlimited supply of thick, green moss on our property. I carefully cover our small foyer table with newspaper and plastic before covering the entire table with moss. Pine cones, tiny sticks, and thick, *safe*, glass votive holders with tea lights inside them finish the display. During the Christmas season, I strategically place a few golden, glassed ornaments onto the earthy moss. Stunning. (You might find artificial moss. Be extra vigilant for any possible fire hazard.)

I also decorate with food. Since winter is the height of citrus season, you will always see a small basket of bright, sunny lemons someplace in our home.

Spring: We move furniture away from windows to let in all the sunshine we can. Fresh new wildflowers or branches with buds fill tall, clear, glass vases. Lilacs are an absolute favorite. I lighten the look of accessories in the spring, when I begin to crave color.

Summer: Our kitchen *groans* under the weight of garden-fresh produce—I decorate with fruits and vegetables. Sure, flowers from our gardens abound, and early summer peonies as big as pie plates are mind-boggling. But walk into our kitchen, and you will see colorful bowls overflowing with summer squash and tomatoes and snap peas and peppers and fresh breads and...oh! I'm missing summer!

Fall: Autumn has to be my favorite season. Bare branches from an outside bush, long stalks of Russian sage, straw flowers scattered on the table, and even a few long, lacy asparagus ferns, one to a jug...and apples and winter squash *everywhere.*

Put Pizzazz in Your Palace

If you are discouraged because decorating dollars are out of the question right now, stick around. You'll have *your* house shouting "Hey, we're glad you're here!" in no time!

This appeared in *Living Well on One Income*, but it bears repeating: Want to put pizzazz in your palace? Jazz up your front door. Keep two thoughts in mind: (1) Presentation is everything, and (2) first impressions go a long way. Stand on the sidewalk and stare at your home: What can you do?

❀ Polish or replace the hardware or the doorknob.

❀ Paint the door. My eye wanders to any home that has a different (and agreeable) color to the front door.

❀ Add a door knocker, or add painted wooden or brass house numbers.

Note from me: Having a well-marked house with numbers easy to read is critical in case of emergency, when fire fighters, police, or paramedics are trying to find you.

❀ Add a doormat. Careful! Some mats trap moisture underneath and rot wood.

❀ Hang a seasonal wreath.

Tag Along!

We have a small, framed verse from the Jewish Talmud hanging just inside our door, and if anything says "howdy," this does: "Hospitality is an expression of divine worship." Our son and his wife have a brass plate that reads: "As for me and my house, we will serve the Lord."

Righteous God, may this house be a haven of peace, a place of safety, and a blessing to all who enter. In Jesus' name. Amen.

Go to the Decorating Pro!

❀ Keep similar things (a collection) grouped for best impact.

❀ Group items of similar color together.

❀ Don't put small items up high, out of sight—unless you have small kids.

❀ Mix things from different periods: Gram's lace hanky, Mom's favorite prayer book, and your modern cup and saucer.

❀ Glue or hang a strip of lace on the edge of your cupboard.

❀ Choose one of the least-used colors in the room to accentuate with accessories.

❀ Change to a crisper, lighter color on walls and cabinets.

❀ Change or paint lampshades.

❀ Change the hardware on your cabinets. (This can be spendy. Can you paint your existing hardware?)

❀ Pictures should hang *barely* above eye level, which is lower in areas where people sit and higher in standing areas, such as hallways.

❀ Need a bookend? Find an awesome rock. Turn finding the rock into a glorious family adventure.

50 Percent!

The top money-saving decorating idea by a *landslide* is to paint. This is one instance in which quality pays off: Better paint is cheaper in the long run. Look for paint with a higher proportion of acrylic solids. Acrylic solids are what make paint durable. Cheaper paints have more water, or filler, and fewer solids. The right *kind* of paint is critical, too.

❀ Home improvement stores offer free seminars and have knowledgeable people to answer your questions. Talk first, paint second.

❀ Small spaces such as halls and bathrooms should have white ceilings and light-colored walls if you want them to look larger.

❀ You can spruce up a small space with crisp white accents.

❀ Yellow is the most popular house color, denoting cheer.

❀ For a cool and relaxing room, opt for blues and creams.

❀ For the warm, hearth-and-home feel, opt for peach, apricot, or gold.

✤ Please give thought before using a bold color. A color that might look terrific with dimmed lights may be hard on the eyes in broad daylight.

✤ One big caveat: Think twice before you paint furniture that may be in its original, natural, wooden glory. Be sure you're not going to regret what you've done...or that you're not permanently wrecking a valuable antique!

Go to the Pro!

Those in the know maintain that color has a direct effect on your mood. Paint experts have explained this to me, pointing out the use of red, for instance, on store signage. (Red means *stop!*) How do you color your world?

Yellow: Good cheer, great thinking color, terrific for rooms where people gather. Too intense, though, in a small space. Not great for bedrooms.

Green: Calming reassurance, healing, good color just about anywhere.

Blue: (Think of water.) Tranquil, thought provoking, super for the bedroom, though you may need to add a warm trim because it is a cool color.

Red: Power all the way. (Think of a politician's tie.) Too stimulating to use a lot. You'd be wise to keep it out of bedrooms and dining rooms, though red accents are awesome according to some decorators.

Orange: Red toned down. Another happy color, orange stimulates and makes you feel upbeat. Even the *smell* of orange stimulates. (Check the colors in fast-food joints.)

Purple: Dignified, royal, and grand. Purple has long been associated with spirituality. Deeper shades might be okay in a bedroom.

Pink: What we women are made of, right? Pink has always been associated with the female gender and is nurturing. Terrific bedroom color.

Try This (for the Small Fry)!

Spiff-up your child's room—and help your child get a sense of organization. Believe it or not, many children like to have their clutter ordered as much as adults do. What can you do?

❀ Use different colors on shelves or drawers to brighten the furniture (great opportunity to use leftover paint).

❀ Get silly with magic markers, stencils, sponges—write names, paint graffiti. Imagine a visiting kid in your child's room, bug-eyed: "Your parents let you paint all over that dresser?"

❀ Turn a headboard into a work of art—or a car or a spaceship.

❀ Create shelves for books, toys, and collections.

❀ Dangle homemade stars from the ceiling with fishing line or dental floss.

❀ Use a large prefab shoe divider as a dresser for toddler's clothes.

50 Percent!

❀ Search thrift stores for awesome tablecloths. Designate part of one closet for your tablecloths, folded and draped over hangers.

❀ Use lengths of florists' ribbon folded over or tied to a dowel as a fluttery covering for the bottom half of a window.

❀ Have an old table that could add a rustic look to your den? Cut down the legs and use it as a coffee table.

❀ Buy good quality used furniture to be way ahead of the game. Used-furniture stores, thrift stores, yard sales, and local classified ads are good places to check.

Note from me: Furniture has an astronomical price markup. Warehouse stores, however, are good places to look when shopping for new.

Extra note from me: Room "ensembles" don't seem to be popular with designers any longer.

Go to the Furniture Pro—Oh, No!

Watch out for ads like this: "No money down, no need to pay us until a Starbucks opens at the North Pole, and not only no interest, but we will pay *you* money just to take home our furniture!"

Remember this maxim: Small print usually takes away what the large print offers. I've read that the actual payment date does not always square with the date you *think* the contract ends, and the interest is retroactive to day one and is sky-high. Your best bet is to stay away from these things. There is no free lunch out there, folks—only gimmicks to look out for.

Try This—Make Your Rental a Home

❀ If the rental came furnished, rearrange the furniture if you may.

❀ Have a nifty quilt or colorful blanket? Use it to cover a drab sofa. Add a few colorful throw pillows.

❀ Surround yourself with *your* things, especially photos of loved ones.

❀ Add bright, colorful throw rugs.

❀ Give yourself instant landscaping with terra-cotta pots filled with flowers, or grow a small garden.

Tag Along!

My life would be a bit sorry without the use of baskets. I tote things in them, store things in them, grow things in them, and present things in them. They serve as magazine racks, kitchen drawers, and linen closets for me. I haul them to farmer's markets and to my own garden. And they are perfect gifts! So here's a tip: Look for sturdy baskets that have handles that go all the way into them, not flimsy handles that are merely attached on the top. The best time to buy is off-season: after Christmas and Easter.

The Tale of a Bad Day

Furious from what you consider a total rip-off at the health food store, you drop the so-called "health" muffins in the slushy snow as you try to balance Precious on your hip outside the preschool. Back into the car she goes, wide-eyed that she is free to crawl unrestrained, while you try to clean the muffins on your parka. Once the muffins are reassembled, you have to crawl into the back of your minivan to retrieve your daughter, who loses a boot and starts wailing. You split the ugliest muffin with her, just to shut her up. Raisin pieces get stuck in your teeth. You don't care because you are famished.

Once inside the door, Junior throws himself at your legs, leaving you with two options: Drop your daughter or drop the muffins. (They said *healthy*, they never said *clean*.)

During the meeting you look at other mothers, who seem to be cool and collected, and you hate them. *They must have nannies, and they aren't wearing sweats.* Your children are the only clingy ones. You offer sensible suggestions while bouncing Precious and discreetly trying to scrape dried snot off your shoulder. Guilty again, you volunteer for the annual fundraiser, regretting your words the second they leave your mouth.

Junior and Precious on board, you head to the video store to plead your case, and you end up buying closeout videos, the boxes of which Precious chews. Your credit card denies the charge. This sends you into spasms of terror, not to mention embarrassment in front of the store clerks, as you step aside and return slobbery videos to their shelves. You know the checking account balance is low. Now this. And you need groceries. Panic.

Not to worry: Another card came in the mail last week. You'll just run home and get it. Once home, you listen to phone messages. Your husband is also feeling guilty about the shirt incident and wants to compensate by bringing home Thai tonight. You think about the finances, but frankly, you just don't care. You owe it to yourself to have this little treat.

Missy called and plans to spend the evening with friends. The day is starting to look up.

To be continued...

11
Conserving Stuff

*O*nly an unusual book, indeed, would discuss the seven deadly sins as well as light bulb wattages. But if you are looking for an effortless way to cut costs, be wise—utilize!

We all use utilities such as electricity, gas, and water daily, and we pay for that use. We also pay for waste removal. And any way we define it, we waste an awful lot.

No More Lip Service

I was on the campus of the University of Montana with a friend. Everywhere we looked, we saw students smoking. This after constant education on the bad effects of smoking since they were in diapers.

"So much for education," I said wryly. Chalk one up to...what? Human nature? Rebellion?

To what do we chalk up our waste of resources? Don't we understand that we pay for every second that a light is left on, for every drop of water that runs needlessly down the drain, for our careless abuse of energy?

This chapter hits us right in our thermostats and reminds us of our responsibility for the good use and care of creation. We are to be faithful stewards in our God-ordained dominion over all things, and no one should suffer from our abuse.

Look at it this way. If a neighbor left for two weeks and asked you to watch her house and water her plants, would you go there and have a wild party, eat everything in the refrigerator, and throw dirt on the walls? What if a mighty, holy God left an entire *planet* in your care?

He did.

There are so many tips, facts, and figures in this category, we're going to roll up our sleeves, go to the pros, and start taking better care of this planet by being resourceful in our own homes.

Go to the Electric Pro!

❀ Three kitchen appliances that are heavy electricity users are the stove, the refrigerator (especially auto-defrost), and the chest freezer.

Note from me: Let me get this straight. You not only have a freezer crammed with food you do not eat, but you're paying serious money to keep that freezer cold, right?

❀ Three kitchen appliances that are low users are your clock, your garbage disposal, and your Crock-Pot.

❀ Three big users in the house are heaters, air conditioners, and the water heater. A water bed and the clothes dryer are close behind.

Note from me: Never again let hot water run needlessly. Might as well straddle the sink and stuff pennies down the drain. Men should fill a small basin with hot water for shaving or use the stopper in the sink. Keep showers reasonably short. When washing dishes, fill the sink with sudsy dishwater on one side and clear rinse water on the other.

❀ Three lowest users: vacuum, sewing machine, and DVD player.

50 Percent!

❀ When used wisely, lighting consumes about 6 percent of an average home's energy costs.

❀ Newer, energy-saving bulbs are expensive on the front end but save bundles over time. (Good source: warehouse store.) Standard incandescent bulbs lose as much as 90 percent of energy as heat. Dust the tops of bulbs (when they're not on) to increase efficiency by 100 percent.

❀ Replacing a 75-watt incandescent bulb with an 18-watt compact fluorescent bulb saves about 570 kilowatt hours over its lifetime. That's over $30 in electricity saved, with the same amount of light.

❀ Higher-watt bulbs are usually more efficient than lower-watt ones—but use them intelligently. Putting a 100-watt bulb in your closet wouldn't make much sense.

❀ If a fixture uses several bulbs, use one higher-wattage bulb rather than several smaller-wattage ones, but never exceed the fixture's recommended bulb size.

❀ Use fixtures with three-way switches; use dimmer switches.

❀ Turn off lights when they're not in use.

❀ Make your home energy efficient with lighter colors. Dark colors absorb light.

❀ Use reflectors in light fixtures. They can double the amount of light.

❀ Use outdoor lights only when needed.

❀ Turn off fans that vent to the outside after cooking or after your shower. One hour's use will expend an entire house's heat to the outside.

❀ Up to 33 percent of a home's heat goes out the windows and doors. You can lose up to 40 percent of your heat if your home is not weatherized.

❀ Air leaks are among the largest sources of energy loss. The most common need for weather stripping is under a door: A quarter-inch gap at the bottom of your door could waste as much warm air as a three-inch hole in the side of your house.

Try This!

Check for air leaks by holding a damp hand near these areas:

chimney	fireplace damper
ceiling fans	attic access
recessed lighting	electric boxes
doors and windows	plumbing

50 Percent!

Utility companies sometimes offer rebates for weather stripping and caulking.

Tag Along!

We use the sun! We take advantage of the sun's heat in winter and keep the intense sun out in summer.

In the summer, we draw shades on windows and close doors that have a direct hit from the sun. This helps keep the home cooler. As the sun moves its way round our home, east shades go up, west shades go down.

The reverse is true in the winter: We keep heavy drapes closed on the north side of the house, and we open south shades and curtains to welcome any free heat from sunshine...sigh...if only the sun would shine in western Montana in the winter!

Go to the Appliance Energy Pro!

❀ Look for Energy Star appliances and ratings.

❀ Side-by-side refrigerator-freezers use more energy than same-sized top-freezer units.

❀ Keep your refrigerator adusted to 36 to 38 degrees and your freezer to 0 to 5 degrees. As little as ten degrees below what is recommended can increase energy use by 25 percent.

❀ Keep your freezer more than three-quarters full for optimum efficiency, but if it's jam-packed, the flow of air is retarded. An understocked freezer is just as bad and merely wastes energy. The refrigerator should allow for air circulation among things.

❀ Open fridge doors as seldom as possible. Don't stand and stare.

❀ Cool cooked foods before placing in fridge.

❀ Do not put uncovered liquids in fridge. They emit vapors that cause condensers to work harder.

❀ Thaw frozen foods in fridge.

❀ Thaw food before cooking. A frozen roast requires as much as 50 percent more cooking time.

❀ Match pots and pans to the diameter of the heating unit. A small pot on a big burner equals wasted energy. A big pot on a small burner uses more energy.

❀ Cook with pans that have clean, flat bottoms.

❀ Use as little water as possible when cooking. Better nutrition, better flavor, better energy consumption.

❀ Keep reflector pans clean on your stovetop. Sigh.

❀ If you use an electric stove, turn off the elements several minutes before the allotted cooking time.

❀ If you use a gas stove, check your flame. The color should be blue for maximum efficiency. If it's yellow, the burner may be clogged with food particles. Clean it with a pipe cleaner.

❀ Do not open the oven while baking or roasting. The temperature could drop 25 degrees.

❀ Maximize your oven use. Try to bake more than one item.

❀ If you use a self-cleaning oven feature, try to do so immediately after oven use.

❀ Self-cleaning ovens use less energy for cooking because of extra insulation.

❀ Convection ovens use about one-third less energy than conventional ovens.

❀ Use microwaves, toaster ovens, and Crock-Pots for small meals.

❀ Keep the lid on! Food will cook faster and at lower temperatures.

❀ HEAT ONLY THE AMOUNT OF WATER YOU NEED FOR A CUP OF TEA. (Just wanted to make sure you saw this, Josh and Joe.)

❀ Dishwashers that use less water use less energy. Water heating accounts for 80 percent of a dishwasher's energy use.

❀ If your dishwasher has a temperature booster, reduce your water heater setting to 120 or 130 degrees. Most people keep their hot water temperature high because of the dishwasher. You might not need to.

❀ Use the short cycle and no-heat drying on your dishwasher.

❀ Operate the dishwasher with a full load. Scrape excess food first, or debris will enter the pump and meddle with efficiency.

❀ Do not run the dishwasher when someone is taking a shower. Balance the hot-water demand.

❀ Wash full loads of clothes unless you can regulate settings.

❀ Do not over-wash clothes.

❀ When washing clothes, use hot water only when necessary. (Using hot water is the only way to kill bedding mites.) Hot water accounts for 90 percent of the washer's energy consumption.

❀ Use cold water rinse when possible.

❀ Front-loading washers use a lot less water and energy.

❀ Dryers with automatic shutoffs save up to 15 percent over dryers with timers.

❀ *Clean the lint filter!*

❀ Operate your dryer with a full load, but do not cram.

❀ Load your dryer with fabrics of similar weight.

❀ Be sure the dryer vent is not clogged.

❀ Use a clothesline if possible. (Slipping between clean sheets that have dried in the sun is a luxury.)

❀ Turn off the TV, radio, and stereo when you're not using them.

❀ Towel-dry your hair before using the hair dryer.

❀ Cover water beds with comforters for insulation.

❀ Do not overload your food disposal.

❀ Audio products consume 90 percent of their energy when they are "off." Using Energy Star qualified products can eliminate 75 percent of that waste.

❀ Turn off appliances when you're not using them. Is your coffeepot still on from this morning?

Try This!

I'm taking this straight from the pages of *1001 Bright Ideas to Stretch Your Dollars:*

Remember the concept of ownership? Get your family involved. Turn this into an energy audit week, followed by a family meeting over tacos or pizza. Ask your local utility if a representative will visit (without charge) to help with energy-saving tips. Build your family meeting around that visit. Display your utility bills and talk about your monthly payments. Prowl around the house, inside and out. Look for places where new weather stripping and caulking could do some serious good. Check all faucets. Read your electric meter every night for a week and discover which day consumed the most energy. Figure out why. Help the kids develop math skills by determining how much electricity all of your small appliances use. Use coins to demonstrate cost or projected savings. Award a prize to the child who conserved the most energy during the week.

Go to the Sanitation Pro!

One way or the other, you pay for trash removal, whether it is in the quality of the water, air, or land, through taxes that keep our landfills running, or through monthly refuse collection fees.

If you pay to visit the refuse center or if you pay a monthly fee for pickup, remember this new word: *precycle.*

Recycling is a terrific habit (some reports claim the energy cost of recycling itself is pretty high), but try to get into the habit of cutting back on refuse in the first place:

❀ Precycle the newspapers. Can you cut back to one? Do you even need that one? Can you read at work, at the library, share with a neighbor, or satisfy your need for news with TV, radio, or the Internet?

❀ Precycle juice and pop containers: Drink water.

❀ Precycle packaging from anything made microwave-ready: Do not buy.

❀ Precycle much in your grocery cart: Buy bulk, bring your own containers, and do not buy individual packaging.

❀ Analyze the contents of your garbage pail to figure how to slash your trash.

❀ Crush your trash before you put it in the pail, especially if you pay for pickup by volume.

Go to the Water Pro!

❀ The average person uses too much water while brushing teeth.

❀ On average, too much water goes down the drain while shaving.

❀ Install a low-flow shower head to reduce water consumption by up to 50 percent.

❀ Leaky faucet? Sixty drops per minute loses 113 gallons per month.

❀ Leaky toilet? You might as well go to the bank for a loan right now.

❀ A plastic one-liter bottle filled with stones and put in your toilet tank (away from the mechanism!) can cut your water use by up to 110 percent. Don't use bricks —they will clog your flusher.

❀ The average automatic dishwasher on full cycle will use 16 gallons. The short cycle uses seven gallons.

Go to the Heating Pro!

❀ The lowest comfortable thermostat setting means the greatest economy. Learn to wear slippers and sweaters. The elderly and young children need a warm room.

❀ Lower thermostats at night.

❀ Thermostats should be on inside walls, away from the drafts of windows and doors.

❀ Do not heat an empty room unless it is plumbed or you have a heat pump.

❀ Keep closet doors shut.

❀ Close the damper on your fireplace when not in use to save up to 8 percent of your heat.

❀ Keep registers, baseboards, and radiators clean and clear of furniture or drapes. Air must circulate for heaters to work at maximum efficiency.

❀ Insulate heating system ducts and pipes. Improperly sealed and uninsulated ducts can waste up to 25 percent of your system's heat.

❀ Keep your heat pump thermostat set on 78 degrees or higher. Each degree you lower it costs about 3 percent more in energy costs.

❀ Wrap your water heater with insulation. (With the correct insulation and installation, you might get an energy rebate.)

❀ In a two-story home in the summer, open the first-floor windows on the shady side and the second-floor windows on the sunny side. Cool air will force warmer air up and out.

❀ Use fans. Have a room that doesn't get enough heat? Put a small fan at ground level pushing air out of the room you want heated. Also, ceiling fans should be in the up mode in summer, down mode in winter.

❀ Bake early or late in the day during hot months.

❀ With an air conditioner, use the "outside air" option only when necessary. Recirculating cool inside air costs less.

❀ Don't install a room air conditioner in direct sunlight.

❀ Plant a leaf-bearing tree on your southwest exposure. Its leaves will block direct sun in the summer, and the bare branches will let the sun warm you in the winter. Plant evergreens on the north and west.

❀ Wrap hot water pipes. Otherwise you'll end up sitting under the house in frigid weather with a blow-dryer in your frozen fingers. And eating old fruitcake.

❀ Keep a bottle of water in the refrigerator to avoid running the tap too long.

❀ Do not cut your lawn short in hot weather.

❀ Water your yard early in the morning.

❀ Always use cold water in garbage disposals.

❀ Use cold water for washing clothes whenever possible.

Tag Along!

Our cable TV cost was around $25 each month—until we called the cable company.

"We don't watch much TV, but want to have a few stations so we can watch newsworthy programs." Surprise. They told us we could get their most basic service (16 channels) for $12 each month. Fine with us.

After all you've just read, now do you believe you can nickel and dime yourself to financial health?

The Tale of a Bad Day

Back to the video store with the two kids. By now you have talked yourself into the new release of a DVD you've been waiting for. Besides, this trip would be almost as embarrassing as your earlier visit if you only charged a few dollars on this brand-new card to buy those soggy closeouts.

On to the grocery. You don't have a drop of milk in the house. And you probably should get some fruit...you *are* trying to serve more nutritious food. At the market, the kids drag you to the bakery. Their excitement over a few cookies is worth any price. You feel especially close to them this afternoon. Maybe the stress of your low checking account balance caused your bad mood. Armed with this new card—which you *promise* you will monitor closely—you are so much happier you buy yourself a bouquet of flowers and a scented candle. And tortilla chips, and dip, and a big bag of chocolate-covered peanuts for Hubby-Dearest. You even buy some of those cute lunches in a box for Missy. And a rawhide treat for Barky.

Colorful flowers on the passenger seat, your spirits are positively buoyed as you drive home. Let's see...straighten the house, and maybe even iron a few shirts. (Talk about permanent press! They've been in the laundry basket so long they're permanently pressed, all right!) You sing along with Raffi and the kids. A block from home you notice the gas light blinking—you are precariously low on gas. As you make a U-turn, you notice Barky out of the corner of your eye and groan at the thought of strewn garbage. You *knew* you should have put that sack of dirty disposables *in* the trash can! How did that dog get out again, anyway?

The closest gas station houses a popular fast-food outlet, and whining in the backseat turns into art form. The children have one thing on their minds, and it will be miserable leaving without it: a Crazy Meal. You relent. Thai is not exactly on their hit parade, anyway. Wanting to cover nutritional bases, you buy them both apple juice to go with their fries.

To be continued...

12
Body Stuff

According to the Statistical Abstract of the United States
Government, the average American woman is around
5 feet 4 inches tall, weighs around 142 pounds, and is
32 years old. Her hips are wider than her shoulders.
She is a stocky size 12.

JAN LARKEY

I'm not sure there is a woman reading this who does not want to feel good and look good—and feel good about how she looks. We spend a lot of money to that end but often end up at a dead-end after rushing to the store or quickly dialing the number on our TV screen to get some new product that will melt pounds, restore zip, smooth away wrinkles, and get rid of grey. (If there really were a product that would melt pounds, I'd stand in a line if it wrapped around the equator! And who doesn't want more energy? I'd even iron wrinkles from my face if I thought I could. And I haven't seen the true color of my hair for so long that for all I know, I'm the Grand Pooh-Bah of Puce by now.)

We women want to look good, and nothing is wrong with that. Our constant care and grooming can feel a bit like cleaning those dusty rooms of ours, but think of the alternative—to let ourselves go to wreck and ruin because, by golly, we *are* going to get old someday. And *(gulp)* die. Why even bother brushing our teeth, combing our hair, or putting our best foot forward? We do it because we like to and because we want to, and so we should. I don't see how we can invest energy and thought into stewardship of other things in our care and overlook our most fundamental possession by not caring for ourselves. We are reminded by Peter, however, that true loveliness comes from *character* that adds immeasurably to our appeal—our glow unmistakable and our smile genuine. But what if we want to outline our smile with red, pink, or coral? What if we want to frame our glow with a pretty haircut? I mean, have you priced lipstick and haircuts lately?

Beauty is a mega-billion dollar business. Merchandisers know us, ladies. All they have to do is promise an amazing result (covered by fine print that usually says, "Results not typical" or "Results vary by individual") and we are all ears. They know the morning will come (about six times each year, I figure) when we look in the mirror and decide we need a haircut, and we mean *now*. When we can't stand our sallow countenance, and we run to the store to get a magic potion *now*. When we are feeling sluggish and can't find energy to get out of bed, and we can be sucker punched by any vitamin or tonic claim, which we buy *now*. In these days of extreme makeovers, add to our impatience the message that worth continues to be measured by appearance. And are we ever excited by the possibilities: Fix my eyes, fix my teeth, fix my nose, fix my chin, fix me! Ever think you are just fine the way you are?

No. I didn't think so. The truth? Me neither. Who wouldn't swoon if one of those reality makeover shows paid a surprise visit? In the meantime, the reality of my life is that if I want to make any improvements—and if I want to make them wisely—I'm going to have to do much myself.

Body Stuff, The Care of

I have taken a long time to figure out my body, and I'm still looking for answers. My advice to you is to not wait until you are well into midlife before you start learning what makes you tick. Do you have allergies? Are you sensitive to some foods? What are your body's weaknesses, and what can you improve? Do you have medical impediments to consider when going about daily routines? Does your family have a predisposition to disease? What *really* is a healthy and realistic weight for you? Are you prone to depression, mood swings, PMS? Are you in the throes of menopause? Connect with yourself. Understand yourself. Visit with your medical practitioner. Read sensible, recommended books. Learn about your body's chemistry, where your organs are and what they do, and the names of your bones. It's *you!* (I did an impromptu survey for this book by stationing myself one morning at Brookies Cookies in Bigfork, Montana. I asked all who walked through the door where their adrenal gland was. Most people thought it was next to their ear and had to do with balance.)

Go to the Health Pro!

❀ Develop a good rapport with your health practitioner. Don't sit there like a dope and nod. Ask questions. Get answers.

❀ Check to see if your community health department sponsors free medical tests, such as well-baby exams, blood pressure tests, and prostate screening.

❀ Call such places as the Salvation Army and inquire about free or low-cost medical and dental clinics.

❀ Free medicine and free medical care are available to qualified applicants. Call the National Association of

Community Health Centers in Washington, D.C.—or the manufacturer of your medication.

❀ Always ask if your doctor has samples of a recommended drug or if generic can be substituted.

❀ If you take steamy showers, vitamins and prescription drugs may not fare well in your medicine cabinet.

❀ We've all heard of the frenzy over Canadian drugs. Their costs are lower because of two factors: Canadian regulatory agencies and the exchange rate.

❀ Warehouse stores often have best prices on drugs. If you have a privately owned pharmacy in town, consider supporting that store.

❀ Private optometrists often beat the prices of big eyeglass chains. Warehouse stores offer eyeglasses as well.

❀ Old glasses can be tinted inexpensively to serve as sunglasses as long as your prescription has not changed. Otherwise, buy a good pair of clip-ons and make your regular glasses do double duty.

❀ Look for appealing frames at eyeglass stores' seasonal closeouts or at thrift stores.

❀ Check for sales around holiday seasons, which are sometimes an industry slump.

❀ Do not upgrade your hearing aid unless it is not working for you.

❀ Hearing aid personnel wear white coats to give the impression they are doctors. They are not. Go to a reputable firm only. Visit a senior center and chat with the people. Find out which firm is patient and willing to help most during the adjustment period.

❀ Large franchisers often have more expensive hearing aids, partly because the customer is paying for national advertising.

❀ A good hearing-aid contract should have a trial period with a return policy.

❀ Those tiny hearing aids that hide in your ears? Vanity.

❀ Do your level best to get to the dentist for a checkup and cleaning once each year.

❀ Replace your toothbrush regularly. And floss your teeth. Flossing will cut down on a potentially big bill later on from gum disease.

❀ Calcium-rich food is extremely important for our teeth. Why is sugar so bad? Bacteria flourish in sugar, and over time the bacteria bore into teeth like one of those dental drills. Sticky foods are worse than sweet foods.

❀ For some reason, cheese seems to help prevent cavities.

According to a dentist named William Kuttler, you should chew more. See? I told you! The more you chew, the more saliva washes away sugars from the teeth. And saliva contains calcium, which neutralizes acids.

Stopwatch!

Cut down waiting room time. Try to land the doctor's first appointment of the day.

Try This!

Smile and laugh. (After you brush, of course.) You will improve your health and your looks. Smiling is an instant face-lift, and laughter releases endorphins into the brain that improve your overall sense of well-being.

50 Percent!

Check with your doctor—many drugs cost the same at higher doses. See if you can invest in a higher dose and cut it in half for a true 50 percent savings.

I've encouraged you to DITCH the diet and to become informed. Most of us have a favorite "health guru." I have three: Jean Carper, whom I've already mentioned, Dr. Andrew Weil, and Dr. Sidney Baker, whose book *The Circadian Prescription* has answered many questions for me. I've learned much from all three and have adapted my lifestyle habits to many of their suggestions. I hope that you will visit your library and find books from them and from others whose suggestions make sense for you.

Tag Along!

I've shared a typical morning in the kitchen. Follow me now as I bring you into my morning routine after breakfast:

If anything is holistic, health is—body, mind, and spirit. Maintaining spiritual health is vital for a disciple of Jesus Christ. Taking the time to commune with God is called many things in Christian circles: Bible study, prayer time, quiet time. My "quiet time" has varied through the years. Sometimes I awoke at 5:30 in order to sit and meditate on God's Word. Other times I drifted away from discipline and was lucky to *think* of praying, let alone do it. For the most part, my practice is to have "quiet time" after our early breakfast. After supplication and Bible study, I turn to my physical body.

I try to remember to take several deep breaths through my nose, hold them, and then expel them fast through my mouth. I do this because bodies need oxygen, and I tend to be a shallow breather. Many mornings, I fill the tub with ankle-deep cold water and "tread" for five minutes. During this time I recite Bible verses I'm trying to commit to memory. *(B...b...b...bless the L...l...lord, O...m...m...my ssssoul...)* I know this sounds insane, but I read someplace that this improves the immune system (It sure wakes me up!) I use a dry brush on my skin most mornings, brushing only in one direction, always toward the heart. The skin is our largest organ. I try not to forget that.

Try This!

It is in the quiet proclamation of mountains that I hear the voice of God thunder. The earth declares His glory all right, in reverent silence.

In this numbing and stimulating world of ours, have you ever embraced silence? When I learned about this gift from God, I really began to listen through soundless, contemplative thought and prayer. My heart connected to stillness and peace that grows daily. To me, silence is one of God's most extravagant gifts. Be still, and know that He is God.

Body, mind, spirit: Try to work toward holistic balance in your life this week.

Speaking of Works...

I am utterly convinced that colon health is an overlooked but crucial element for health *and* beauty. If you are sluggish in this department, water, exercise, and natural aides should be utmost on your "to do" list. Few of us get enough fiber, drink enough water, and eat enough prunes.

Beauty and Exercise
Try This!

Take the time to round up all of your beauty products and paraphernalia. I'd wager you'll find eye shadow from ten years

ago, more futile stabs at your perfect lipstick color than you
care to admit, and enough lotions to fill a five-gallon bucket.
Get rid of all the old stuff. It's probably laden with harmful bacteria by now anyway. Pare down to what you really use. Now
look at it. You may be looking at your makeup palette, the
result of all of your experimentation over the years. Use what
you have before you spring for something new (unless it is
rancid, of course).

Go to the Hair Pro!

❀ Salon shampoos are highly concentrated. Use less.

❀ Big bottles of shampoo seem to be a bargain, but water
is often the main ingredient.

❀ Many hair conditioners, particularly cream rinses,
cause wax buildup. If this happens, wash with a mixture of water and either vinegar or lemon juice.

❀ Salon services are expensive because you are paying
for overhead and ego gratification.

❀ Try to find a stylist who can fashion the best look for
your face. Pay for that look, and then find a capable
person to maintain the style at a lesser cost.

❀ Find a beauty salon that will trim your neck and bangs
between cuts for free.

❀ At-home hair coloring can be an inexpensive alternative if you do it right, pick the right color, and pick a
coloring agent that is compatible with your hair and
complexion.

❀ If an all-one-length hairstyle looks attractive on you,
adopt it to avoid haircuts.

❀ Highlight blond hair with 1/4 cup of lemon juice in 3/4 cup of water. Use olive oil to condition dry, brittle hair.

❀ Invest in a pair of shears and cut the family's hair yourself—unless you are like me. I took an electric razor to our son when he was little. Route 66 right up the back of his head. Family members run screaming when I walk into a room with scissors.

Go to the Beauty Pro!

❀ You do not need to spend a fortune on facial moisturizers. Merchandisers know how badly we want to reclaim our youth, and they will make all kinds of promises. Keep your face clean, keep yourself healthy, eat well, use a quality moisturizer from a big box discounter or a warehouse store, stand tall, and smile.

❀ Tone down that bright red lipstick mistake with a lighter shade over the top.

❀ Make your lips look bigger by putting a dab of gloss or a dab of a lighter shade on the middle of your bottom lip.

❀ Lip liners should be neutral, or the same color as your lipstick.

❀ Eyebrows are like punctuation on the face. Are yours exclamation points, question marks, or commas?

❀ A bit of darker shade under the cheek bone makes the face thinner.

❀ Pink blush gives a healthy glow regardless of your skin color.

❀ Round face? Wear earrings longer than they are wide.

✸ Long, narrow face? Wear square or round earrings, no dangles.

✸ Square face? Wear round or oval earrings, hoops, and buttons.

50 Percent!

✸ With no offense meant to the lady who hands you a small catalogue *every month, what are you doing?* Go look at that pile of makeup and beauty products you just pared down. Stop, already. Support that lady, but only buy what you need.

✸ Need a massage? Go to the school where therapists are trained. Bet you can get one for half price. Also check for an aesthetician's school near you for a good bargain on facials.

✸ For an inexpensive alternative to buying dumbbells, use two empty half-gallon milk jugs (with handles) filled with water or sand. (One gallon of water equals eight pounds.)

Increase Your Love Life by 50 Percent!

Use your perfume.

Tag Along!

After lots of false starts, I have settled on two methods of exercise. One is a stretching regimen called Pilates. I find that when I do my morning "beginner Pilates," my body feels more lithe, and back pain is history. Having memorized the routine, I need not watch the video and can breeze through my exercise in less than 15 minutes.

Walking is my other exercise. My goal is to walk ten thousand steps each day. When I am busy, I rarely meet my goal.

The part of our year spent in Virginia offers unlimited walking opportunities. Joe, Jill, and I walk cobbled streets in and out of Jeffersonian history. In Montana our walking routine is more rugged.

Ten Awesome Things to Do While Walking

1. Greet those you meet with a grin. Wave to merchants.

2. Explore a new neighborhood.

3. Try to cut time from your established route, or to go farther every day.

4. Pick up litter.

5. Breathe deeply. (Unless you are in heavy traffic.)

6. Swing your arms briskly—it's called "cross crawl" and is good for the body.

7. Take the dog. To a dog, a walk is like going to a rock concert. Pick up after your dog.

8. Pray as you commune with God's creation.

9. Discover something new every day.

10. Listen to a book on tape.

50 Percent!

Keep something in mind: Walking is free, and movement is health.

Your Body, The Clothing of

Go to the Retail Pro!

✵ Get familiar with the "Retail Dateline." Start watching for spring clothing closeouts around the last week in April. Watch for any holdover spring clothing, as well as all summer clothing, to close out around the last week in July. Most fall and all back-to-school clothes should close out around the end of October, and winter and holiday clothes get slashed around the end of January.

- "Clean Up in Season" means items with a seasonal application must be sold during that season or holiday time. Think of red and pink hearts on under-thingies—on February 15.
- A good department store will be out of seasonal merchandise at the peak of the season. If you wait for "out of stock" price slashing, the nice selection will be long gone. However, retailers reduce prices dramatically on goods that have lingered beyond the peak selling period.
- "Specials" are usually sales for items seldom or never carried before. Traditionally, the quality is poorer than normal merchandise. Men's flannel shirts that sell two for $12 or so are an example.
- Just about everything in a clothing store will go on sale for 25 percent off sometime during its life.
- "Clearance" or "Red Tag Sales" means the goods are being reduced permanently. The first clearance markdown is usually 30 percent. Fifty percent is the magic number for good buys.
- Avoid high traffic areas, where retailers prey on impulse buyers. The best sales are found in the back of the department.
- If you shop in a thrift store, look for quality. Read labels. Look twice. Why is the garment in the thrift store? Is it stained? Does it require time-consuming care?

50 Percent!

❊ Go to rummage sales or garage sales—especially in upper-crust neighborhoods. But please...you will be tempted to buy much more stuff at these sales than you need.

❊ Do not buy a new wardrobe. Accessorize what you have.

❊ Swap clothes with friends or relatives, especially if you have children.

❊ Avoid unnecessary catalog buying. Catalog buying is usually more expensive, and you can't try anything on. The shipping and handling will kill you. I once bought a long black corduroy shirtdress from a catalog. When I put it on I looked like a Greek olive with feet.

Midwinter savings on outerwear can soar as high as 75 percent off. How can you tell if you are getting a good deal?

❊ Look at the lining. A wide band of outside fabric inside the coat indicates quality; a narrow band indicates a lower quality garment.

❊ Stay clear of designer labels. A non-designer coat will keep you just as warm.

❊ Synthetic filling can often save you up to 25 percent over down fill.

❊ This is an awesome time to buy next year's Christmas presents.

❊ Women's shoes go on clearance sales in February and July...up to 75 percent. (Buy shoes late in the day, when your feet have spread out.)

Go to the Maternity Pro! (That sounds odd...)

❀ The worst times to shop are March, September, and October.

❀ Look for end-of-season deals in January and February for winter clothes, and in July for summer clothes.

❀ Check sweats and shirts in the men's department.

❀ Buy oversized non-maternity clothes.

❀ Look for separates: elastic waists, baby-doll dresses, oversized tunics, and leggings that expand.

❀ Accessorize using colorful scarves, a cool hat, bracelets, and comfortable shoes.

Clothes, The Care of

Go to the Dry Cleaning Pro!

No! Don't! Your clothes will be loaded with bad chemicals! If you get something dry-cleaned, air it out!

❀ What is dry cleaning? The dry cleaner marks and sorts your clothes on the basis of color and type of material and then puts them in a machine. The dry cleaning machine is like a washing machine, but it uses solvents instead of water. (These solvents are bad for you to breathe or have next to your skin.) After clothes go though the machine, the operator removes stains. Next comes pressing.

❀ Don't try to remove stains yourself unless you know what you are doing. Old stains are harder to remove.

❀ Ask if the cleaner will make minor repairs as part of the cleaning cost. Many cleaners offer some services for free.

❀ Don't get same-day service unless absolutely necessary. Same-day-anything costs more.

❀ Don't wash clothes and then take them to the cleaners for ironing.

Stopwatch!

Take permanent press items out of the dryer at once. Hang or fold immediately.

50 Percent!

❀ Your clothes will last longer if you keep them out of the dryer.

❀ Your clothes will fade less if you wash them inside out.

❀ Ring around the collar? Shampoo dissolves body oils.

❀ Cut fabric softener sheets in half.

❀ Extend clothing life by ironing knee patches inside children's pants for longer wear.

❀ Get a good book on stain removal.

❀ Avoid "dry clean only" clothing. Rayon doesn't hold up well and usually needs dry cleaning.

❀ Avoid 100 percent cotton shirts; they do not hold their press. Linen? Only if you don't mind ironing!

❀ Save old shoes for doing yard work. Ever cut your grass wearing new sneakers? *That* was an "oops" moment, huh?

Clothes, The Wearing of

50 Percent!

❀ Create a vertical look. Try to keep one color scheme from head to toe.

❀ Women's clothing should hug their curves a *bit*. I took a long time to figure this out: Baggy clothes hang from our body's widest points and make us look dumpy.

❀ Cuffs on slacks and trousers make people look shorter.

❀ Models choose clothing that is just a *bit* big for them. (Not baggy.) Makes them look slimmer.

❀ Side pockets on women's pants and skirts accentuate hips.

❀ Don't put delicate shoes on clunky feet or clunky shoes on delicate feet.

Try This!

Recycle, rearrange, and revitalize your wardrobe. Create new outfits out of the clothes, accessories, and jewelry you already have. This is a twist on the "use things up" concept. You probably have dozens of possibilities if you mix and match what you already own.

The Tale of a Bad Day

Though somewhat hectic, your evening is quite pleasant even though you ended up with the unhappy task of cleaning the strewn trash left by Barky, who is happily gnawing on her rawhide bone. Past history tells you this will make her vomit, but her pleasure now is worth the cleanup. In spite of her aggravating habits and expensive upkeep, she is such a sweet dog.

Missy surprises everyone by coming home early due to "gross" food at her friend's, so you are faced with making dinner after all. Not to worry. A call to the pizza joint will solve that. Why should she be stuck with macaroni and cheese on treat night for everyone else?

You hear the door and know Hubby-Dearest is back with take-out. Unfortunately, Barky already had a fitful stomach— in the foyer—and your keenly anticipated Thai soup goes flying as Hubby slips on her deposit and wrenches his back. Everyone runs for towels, which you remember are still in the washer. One quart of cellophane noodle soup can do mighty damage in a small area: It has covered the floor, the walls, the carpeted stairs, and the huge pile of shoes and boots. Two rolls of paper towels later, the mess is clear except for a noodle dangling from the light fixture, which you will get sometime later. Sure.

Hubby-Dearest is on the couch with a bag of frozen peas on his back, when Missy announces her science project is due tomorrow. Precious has nodded off over a piece of pepperoni pizza, and Junior has already begun his nightly bedtime snit.

While you are looking for pieces of Tinkertoys to construct Missy's project, you eye the flowers you bought earlier. In a vase, all right, but no water! Running to the sink with your droopy bouquet, *you* slip on a slobbery piece of rawhide and skid into the high chair. This causes Precious to wail, Junior and Missy to laugh, Barky to bark, and your husband to call out, "You okay?"

You explode. Everyone disappears, except for Hubby-Dearest, who magically appears in the kitchen once he figures out his back is not as painful as he thought.

Precious in one arm and Junior in tow, you stomp upstairs leaving your husband to build an atom with your daughter. By the time the two young ones are in bed, you are famished and want to sink your teeth into something sweet.

The rest of this tale bears a striking similarity to that of our first mother.

13
Fun Stuff

Recreate: *to give new life to*

Jesus: *"I am the way, the truth and the life..."*

Fun, The Having of

What finer way to end a book on better living than to talk about recreation. I like the meaning of that word: new life. I hope that I have helped in some small way to make yours a fresher, newer, and better life.

Many of us must deconstruct our thinking about fun. (That is, if we ever think about fun in the first place.)

I've already campaigned for us to bring back the Sunday table and to come together as families and as communities. Let me add to that appeal the notion of play. If you don't know what that means, watch some kids. They can teach us all a few things.

We don't play anymore. We don't play for all of the reasons I've been harping about in this book: stress, push, our dumbing-down and numbing-down, money problems, health issues. Also, I'm not so sure we know how.

I miss play. Play evokes the memory of pleasure, of laughter, and of fun. The delight of play is that it really can't be done alone. It requires community, fellowship, and friendship.

227

Away from the solo computer game! Away from zoning out in front of television! Away from that latest spy thriller! Go do something fun with someone! And by doing, celebrate the fact that you are alive, that you are breathing, that you have the freedom to walk in rusty fall leaves or in snow up to your knees, and that you can huff and puff to run to first base or make a fool of yourself playing charades.

My underlying goal has been for you to fully grasp biblical principles as you manage your affairs and turn to simpler times. My final goal is to encourage you to enjoy yourself in the process. Many forms of recreation don't involve investing a fortune in equipment or toys. The best part about fun is that it can be free.

50 Percent!

❀ Check Friday's newspaper for weekend and weeklong events, check church calendars, check your local college for free lectures, check bulletin boards.

❀ Volunteer to usher at local theater productions and watch the play for free.

❀ Call local firms and ask if they will give your family a tour or demonstration.

❀ Go to the library! Designate a library night for the entire family. Don't just borrow books; borrow music, videos, and magazines.

❀ Rediscover reading out loud as recreation, and include children.

❀ Declare a Spanish week and learn as much as you can about Spain. Put an ad in the local paper and ask if anyone from Spain is living in the area. Invite that person to dinner and learn from each other. Then do Ireland, Australia, Bolivia, Uganda...

- Plant a garden. Assign everyone a particular crop.
- Cook together. Write a family cookbook with a certain theme and give it as a Christmas gift. Illustrate with family photos and children's art.
- Host a scavenger hunt. We've turned loose teams looking for Polish catechisms, tutus, water from Niagara Falls, basset hounds, red linoleum...

Try This (for the Small Fry)!

- Challenge the kids to create a mini golf course in your backyard.
- Challenge the kids to *create* a backyard. Give them each a certain amount to spend on seeds or plants at the nursery. Help them with creativity—show them how a few rocks in a circle can define a garden space. Show them how to group lawn furniture to define a sitting space. Teach them to use resources on hand.
- Make Rice Krispies treats but have the kids cut them into shapes and decorate with sprinkles. Use cocoa-flavored Rice Krispies for variation.
- Purchase a disposable camera. Present it to a child, along with a notebook. Tell the child to write a book about the week and to illustrate with photos.
- Host a tower-building contest. See who can build the highest tower with marshmallows and sturdy spaghetti.
- Decorate a straw hat with buttons and bows. Get crazy. (If using a glue gun, you handle it to keep children from being burned.)
- Help the kids empty their closet. Have them put on old clothes. Give them several paint colors and brushes of

all sizes. Protect the floor. Challenge them to turn the inside of their closet into whatever they choose: mural, graffiti, or a theme, such as stars, clowns, or horses. Turn the closet into the bottom of the sea, the inside of a volcano, the top of a mountain. You can paint over it when they are old and grown, but why would you want to?

❀ Gather old jeans, a flannel shirt, a big old belt, an old pair of work shoes, and a scarf. Gather straw or rags (or a ton of plastic grocery sacks) and make a scarecrow. Be creative with the head—stuff an old pillowcase and draw a face. Seat the scarecrow in a lawn chair on your front porch. Better than a pumpkin.

Try This Olympic Idea!

Organize a Summer Olympics for your neighborhood. Here's what to do:

❀ Create a few committees: awards presentation, games, parade, promotion. Keep all of this fun and low-key.

❀ Meet a few times and discuss your progress: Can a couple of dads make a creative maze or obstacle course for the youngsters? Is someone able to help the kids decorate bikes and wagons (and Labrador retrievers) with balloons and streamers? Can you find a few lonely oldsters who might thoroughly enjoy "judging" the events with fat-tipped magic markers and pieces of cardboard?

❀ Can you creatively invent new categories? Think of country picnics and fairs, of Olympic events, of pet shows, and craft shows. Design competitions to fit the kids who will participate. The youth pastor of a local church would have plenty of ideas. Youth pastors have balanced tons of eggs on spoons and run in zillions of three-legged races—and executed more flips and flops than Michelle Kwan.

❋ Organize a neighborhood Summer Olympics with a twist: Ask everyone to include their pets. (As long as the pets don't bite.)

Try This Outdoor Fun!

❋ Stay up very late and learn about the stars. Get a guidebook from the library.

❋ Get up very early, make a thermos of hot chocolate or mint tea, and go as a family to a nearby lake, lock, ocean, river, stream, reservoir, pond, or puddle. Sit and sip tea and watch the world awaken. Please try to do this. It will be a memory your children will cherish.

❋ Watch the papers for any free outdoor concerts.

❋ Go for a hike in a new neighborhood. Look for ideas to take home: interesting paint combinations, gardens, landscaping, mailboxes.

❋ Paint your mailbox. Make it fun. Put everyone's name on the outside.

❋ If you have an old cemetery nearby and if you aren't trespassing or being disrespectful, make gravestone rubbings. Then wonder out loud together about the people's lives.

❋ Gather pinecones with the children. Roll the cones in peanut butter and then in birdseed. String outside on trees...as long as you do not live in bear country. If I did this, I'd have a visit from a grizzly for sure!

Try This Rainy Day Fun!

❀ Get enough copies of a certain play from a library for all the family members. Then act out the play, reading from the script. (Shakespeare, maybe?)

❀ Once and for all—go to that museum or art gallery in town. Get dressed up before you go.

❀ Show up at a hospital or nursing home and ask if you can do anything to help.

❀ Go to the bank for coin wrappers. Teach the kids to count and to save by filling wrappers with pennies and nickels and dimes and quarters.

❀ Make a miniature golf course in your living room. Use oatmeal boxes, cups, boards, books. Use an upside-down umbrella as a club.

❀ Invent a new soup together. Get bold with herbs and spices—they probably need to be used anyway.

❀ Write a story. Create characters with funny names; turn it into a mystery. Our Ellen keeps bugging me to write a story called *The Candle of Gloom.* Maybe I'll do that once this book is finished...

❀ Build a fort by draping blankets and sheets over furniture. A card table works best. Crawl in with the kids. Bring treats.

❀ If the child is old enough and if you supervise, carve a bar of soap. Start with something easy, like the *Leaning Tower of Pisa.* Then learn about it.

❀ Invent a board game around your family's history.

50 Percent!

Ever see children's floor mats advertised in catalogs? They have roadways, towns, obstacles, and signs drawn all over. The idea is that kids can play on them with their toy cars. Bet you could make your own with magic markers, tape, and other supplies. Why not draw a town that includes your child's very own neighborhood and home? Use a piece of plastic or canvas.

We pay over $20 billion each year on toys. Want my two-cents? Most of those billions go to the landfill, are played with briefly and then discarded, or end up in the attic or cellar. Here are a few facts:

❀ Exceptional sales on toys are extremely rare.

❀ Toys do not follow a sales season, but seasonal sales can be good if you buy summer toys in winter and vice versa.

❀ Toys are usually legitimate end-aisle sale items. Called an "end cap," big discounters will sometimes display popular toys as loss-leaders.

❀ A discount of 25 percent is a good markdown for toys.

And when buying toys for grown-ups...

❀ Buy sporting equipment used until you know you will truly embrace the sport. Without a doubt, the exercise and sporting equipment you want is languishing in someone's basement. Put an ad in the paper or watch the ads.

❀ Go to a pro shop and ask if you can buy a demo.

❀ Buy sporting goods at swap meets, yard sales, and off-season sales.

234 @ Ditch the Diet and the Budget

❀ Many golf courses give discounts to golfers willing to play early or late in the day.

Travel

Watch out! Responsibilities can stand as roadblocks to rest and recreation and can keep that vacation just ahead of you indefinitely. You *can* travel without taking out a loan, even if you have to sleep on that uncomfortable bar across your friend's sleeper couch for a night or two. Inexpensive travel usually means one thing, however: the family car.

Travel by car cuts expenses dramatically. Beside savings, you have the freedom to stop and go as you please. Lines at air or train terminals are eliminated, as is the shuttle to your motel. With a car you can usually go straight to your destination.

Before you travel by car...

❀ Study a map and check all available routes. Know in advance where you can buy gas or make potty stops.

❀ Buy only gas at pit stops. Bring your own treats.

❀ Exception: Let dessert be a frozen treat on a stick at the next pit stop.

❀ Look for big trucks in the parking lot. They are a sure sign of inexpensive food.

❀ Learn about your route. Take detours. Leave the interstate every now and then to visit a museum, enjoy a vista, or swing in a park.

❀ Make sure you thoroughly check your car: tire condition and inflation, fluids, and belts. Keep water and oil in the trunk along with flares, a blanket, and a first-aid kit.

✿ Boredom is a factor, especially for children. Plan to play a few games, such as license plate bingo.

✿ A swimming pool is an answered prayer for people traveling with children. Find the least expensive motel with a pool and be certain the pool is open and operating. If there is no pool, does the town where you are staying offer public swimming accommodations?

✿ Unless you are tent or trailer camping, you need to develop motel savvy before you hit the road.

Go to the Towing Pro!

If your car breaks down while traveling...

✿ If you are near a small town, go to a café frequented by locals. Ask the waitress for coffee and then ask, "Who's the best mechanic in town?"

✿ In a large city, check with the local parts distributor for a good mechanic.

✿ Emergency tows can be expensive. If you are doing any serious traveling, you might want to join an auto club. Some extended warranty contracts cover towing, as do some insurance policies. Be aware of the towing benefit limit.

50 Percent Your Motel Costs!

✿ Always ask, "Is that your lowest rate?"

✿ Motels often cost more in resort or metropolitan areas.

✿ Big city hotels usually cater to business people during weekdays and often have super rates on weekends.

❀ Resorts are usually busiest on weekends. A midweek visit might be thrifty.

❀ "Kids stay free" means nothing if you are paying a high price in comparison to other motels.

❀ Tell the clerk you have a limited budget, and ask for help to keep costs down. (Ownership.) Can you add cots? Can you put small children on the floor in sleeping bags?

❀ Do not order room service!

❀ Do not make calls from your room phone. Go to the public phone in the lobby, or use your cell as long as you won't pay roaming fees.

❀ Do not eat or drink anything from the motel mini-fridge.

❀ Sometimes a motel might be less costly than staying with friends if you feel obliged to reciprocate by taking your friends out to dinner.

Try This!

❀ Colleges, organizations, and churches regularly offer travel deals.

❀ Host a foreign exchange student—bring a country to your home.

❀ Stay with a friend or relative, but remember that this offer works both ways.

❀ Trade homes for a few weeks with someone from another state or country. Do this through a reputable service agency.

❀ Send the kids to Gram's for the night…a vacation in itself!

❀ Try elder or youth hostels. Watch your belongings!

❀ Rent a motor home for a few days.

❀ Pitch in with another couple and rent a cabin. State parks offer good deals.

❀ Go camping. Some stores sell tents large enough to sleep a family for the cost of one night's motel.

50 Percent!

Organize a travel club. Get together with other families and friends. Pick one country each month and assemble together after all have researched the "destination." Serve ethnic food, wear ethnic clothing, and practice different customs. Go to your library or travel agent to borrow a video about your "destination." Travel as far as your creativity will take you. And if you do actually travel abroad…

❀ Rail Europe has a Europass that provides a discount when two people travel together: buy one, the second is 50 percent off.

❀ Go to busy places *off* season. Shorter lines and lower prices compensate for poor weather.

Try This!

You don't have to travel far and wide to experience new things. Tour your own town. You don't have to unpack dirty laundry, you sleep in your own bed, and you don't tire yourself out.

❊ Gather interesting brochures from your Chamber of Commerce for ideas.

❊ Read newspapers, especially the entertainment sections.

❊ Read and study tour books that cover your part of the state.

❊ Study maps (this is fun!) and try to find roads you've never been on.

❊ Pay close attention to fraternal, church, or benevolent organizations when they post their bazaars, potlucks, harvest dinners, and pancake breakfasts.

Fun: The Celebrating of Others

Hearing that Jesus had silenced the Sadducees, the Pharisees got together. One of them, an expert in the law, tested him with this question: "Teacher, which is the greatest commandment in the Law?"

Loving, cherishing, and celebrating others is the most fun of all.

Jesus replied: "'Love the Lord your God with all your heart and with all your soul and with all your mind.' This is the first and

greatest commandment. And the second is like it: 'Love your neighbor as yourself.' All the Law and the Prophets hang on these two commandments" (Matthew 22:34-40).

Are you, like me, happiest when giving, whether a gift or a hug? Would you like to be able to give without breaking the bank, to show your appreciation and affection in a unique manner without stressing about how? Two final segments of this section may help.

Tag Along and Stop the Watch!

Stop the watch is right! Preparing for company takes time.

❀ Depending upon the reason for the visit, I scent our home by simmering essential oils:

⚜ Orange or peppermint for vibrancy and stimulation.

⚜ Rosemary for mental stimulation.

⚜ Clary sage for an evening of pleasant dining.

⚜ And old faithful: lavender for tranquility and a sense of well-being.

❀ I blast through the guest bathroom to quickly freshen.

❀ I put on appropriate music, not too loudly:

⚜ Someone like Neil Diamond for vibrancy.

⚜ Classical music for mental stimulation.

⚜ Jazz for dining.

⚜ Someone like Fernando Ortega for tranquility and well-being.

❀ I go to lengths to be certain our entrance is free from clutter and is itself a hearty welcome to those who enter. This includes the outside entrance.

❀ If preparing a meal, I set our table with care, standing back from the table *many times* to view it with the eye of a guest. I am careful to place candles in such a manner that diners will not burn their arms reaching for food. I consider a side table for bowls and platters if I want to keep the table romantic and clear. I always think of the comfort of company:

- ✫ Can someone easily leave the table if necessary?

- ✫ If someone is left-handed, what is sensible seating?

- ✫ Am I seating people together who aren't too crazy about each other?

- ✫ Have I provided adequate utensils, water, napkins?

- ✫ Is the temperature too hot or too cold? Will the sun glare in someone's eyes?

- ✫ Am I serving foods and beverages consistent with our guest's preferences or beliefs?

- ✫ What time considerations must I keep in mind? Do our guests have to work early? Do they have to drive babysitters home? Do they have medical conditions?

- ✫ In what other ways can I honor the people who will be visiting our home? How can I love my neighbor as myself?

Try This!

Assemble the following: tablecloth, cloth napkins, tea, teapot, teacups, cookies, and sugar cubes. Now think of a friend whom you would like to honor. Host an appreciation tea.

Invite others who would also like to honor your friend. Tell them you are holding a surprise tea party. Ask each to come with a long-stem artificial flower and to be prepared to express why that flower reminds her or him of the person you all admire. (To make the event even more special, have the guests write their sentiments on cards for the honoree to keep.)

Set as pretty a table as you can. Everyone will enjoy sitting and chatting and especially sharing anecdotes and fond memories of time spent with the person. As each person shares reasons for the specific flower selection, she places her flower in a vase you have provided. The person being honored will receive several gifts:

✤ Something we don't get too often: affirmation and appreciation.

✤ A bouquet of several different kinds of flowers, each a reminder of the person who gave it.

✤ A memory that won't quit.

✤ Tea and cookies.

50 Percent!

No one's birthday should go by without a birthday cake. Think of it—a birthday is the most special day of the year for a person. It is his or her very own day. Bake a cake! Or buy a cake at the bread outlet and decorate it. Store-bought cakes are good in a pinch, and one of those big sheet cakes is perfect for a crowd. Decorate a muffin or a donut if that's all you have!

✤ Put a handful of real chocolate chips into a strong, ziplock baggie. Soak the baggie with the chips in very hot water until the chocolate is melted. (When chocolate melts it retains its shape, so you have to mush it a bit.) Cut a tiny tip off the corner of the baggie. Gather the baggie in one hand and squeeze the chocolate out the opening. Drizzle all over the cake. Color outside the lines! Let the chocolate drizzle on the plate. Just zigzag all over.

✤ For a great addition to the chocolate drizzle or a pretty decoration on its own, get a fine strainer and hold it over the cake. Gently shake about half a teaspoon of powdered sugar into the strainer, moving it and shaking it over the cake like fine dust.

❀ Frost the cake. Once frosted, scatter colored sprinkles, curly ribbon, or candies on top and add colored candles. Hint: Put the cake in the freezer first so you have a hard surface to frost. And dip your frosting knife in hot water from time to time.

❀ A nifty idea: After cake is frosted, wrap a ribbon around the base like a hat band. Then cover the top with coconut or with fresh edible flowers.

❀ Use your creative genius! Does your friend like to crochet? Stick a couple of colorful crochet needles into the cake. Does he like to golf? Stick colorful golf tees all over the place.

Ten Ways to Love the One You Love!

1. Remember how you used to have regular eye contact and smile at each other? Do it again.

2. The next time he aggravates the tar out of you, laugh it off and don't take it so seriously. (I know this is hard, but you—and I—can do it!)

3. Stand by the window, watch for him to come home, and then meet him at the door. This is way better than sticking your hand in the air to tell him to hush until you read the last paragraph or watch the last episode of your favorite show.

4. Soak his feet. Then give him a foot massage with warm oil. Use canola if you have to. A foot massage is close to the top of the list of stress relievers and is definitely an act of selfless love.

5. Know what tops the list? A head massage. Run a soft brush through his hair (or lack thereof) and massage his temples. Ever get your hair done? You know the comfort of having your head rubbed.

6. Affirm him in front of others—and mean it.

7. Write a prayer just for him. Talk with your holy God. Thank Him for your mate. Pray for his protection, his health, and his well-being. Show your man the prayer, and pledge to pray it every morning before you even open your eyes.

8. Write a love poem. It doesn't have to rhyme, it can be silly, or it can be mushy. Attach it to a balloon and tie it to his car antenna.

9. Sit him down and tell him *why* you love him.

10. Keep the admonition of the Bible in mind: Husbands, love your wives; wives, respect your husbands.

Try This!

❊ Take dinner to someone in need—a struggling single parent, an elderly couple on a limited income, or a family with someone sick or disabled.

❊ Do you have a friend who is down in the dumps? Go to that person's house and prepare dinner—a Blue Plate Special. After you clean up, play cards, go for a stroll, or sit and listen. Or just sit and be there.

Try This (for the Small Fry)!

Gather some grass seed, potting soil, and a jelly-roll pan. Two or three weeks before Easter, plant the "lawn" with a child. For Easter, place colored eggs, candies, and small tokens of your love on the grass. After Easter, and when the weather permits, plant the sod in a special place on your property. With the child, create a unique border around this plot of land. Perhaps add wildflower seeds, or plant a spring or fall flower bulb.

Fun: The Gifting of Others

As I have mentioned in previous works, we give gifts to honor others for personal accomplishment or life passage, or simply because of feelings of friendship and love. Our gifts bear tidings of goodwill, kindness, praise, and respect. We give because we *want* to give. I've compiled a few lists for you at the end of this book as a sort of gift to you, to help you in a pinch when you wonder what to give and how to present your present.

Go to the Pro! (That would be me. I wrote a book on gift giving.)

Presentation

❋ Try to keep all of your gift-wrapping gear in a designated drawer, cupboard, or one of those plastic shelving units on wheels.

❋ Within reason, keep everything that can be used to wrap a gift: paper from gifts received, tissue paper, leftover fabric, wallpaper...

❋ Wrap gifts in Sunday funnies or in plain newsprint. Red ribbon goes well with newspaper.

❋ Wrap small items with magazine pages.

❋ Keep anything that can be used to adorn a package, a basket, or a jar. Attach a small, inexpensive trinket that hints of the gift. For a cook, tie on a wire whisk.

❋ Paint a wishbone with red nail polish and adorn a gift.

❀ Always have curly ribbon on hand—it gives you unlimited possibilities. No ribbon? Use yarn. No yarn? Use string.

❀ Wrap a house gift in a bright new dish towel.

❀ Keep a couple of baskets of different sizes on hand as containers for any kind of gift. Check thrift stores for baskets.

Baskets

❀ The trick to designing gift baskets is to use one large, inexpensive item to give the look of abundance.

❀ Use double-sided sticky tape or fat packing tape to hold items next to each other. The tape should not be visible.

❀ Fill the bottom of the basket with Easter grass, raffia, Styrofoam packing peanuts, crumbled tissue paper, or newspaper hidden under a piece of fabric or a dish towel. Create height.

❀ Dangle parts of the gift from the basket handle: two cookie cutters tied together with twine, a couple of wooden hearts, or small objects that match what's inside the basket.

❀ Use the standby (raffia) to finish the look.

Generic Gifts

❀ Buy gifts on sale throughout the year. Think ahead. Buy seasonal closeouts.

❀ Buy inspirational books at reduced price. They are perfect for last-minute gift giving. Blank journals are *slashed* right after the New Year. Stock up on these and give them as gifts throughout the year.

❀ Keep a "gift box" into which you put everything from free samples to gift-worthy items, such as coffee mugs. (No—I take that back. I, for one, am growing weary of getting coffee mugs as gifts. How about you?)

❀ Give a traditional Christmas ornament to family or friends. Who cares if the person's birthday is in July? Makes it all the more fun.

❀ Put away a child's favorite toy when interest wanes. Present it when the child is grown.

❀ When in doubt, give food.

❀ If you give the gift of time (such as babysitting), be specific and follow through.

Romantic Gifts

❀ Plant a tree on your anniversary. Watch it grow. Sit under its shade when you are old.

❀ Give each other roses for Mother's and Father's Day. Not the kind that cost as much as your microwave— the kind you plant. Plan your rose garden. Make a rustic arbor out of materials you scrounge up. Plant old roses that climb fences.

❀ Celebrate special days in special ways. Joe and I eat breakfast for dinner on the anniversary of our first meeting—which was at breakfast time.

Tag Along!

Joe and I try to give each other gifts often. We have a white bag with "Isle of View" (I love you) printed on it. The holder of the sack is responsible to ante up the gift. We give things like favorite candy bars, love notes, or flowers. We try to "sneak" our sack attack to add mystery and surprise.

Try This (for the Small Fry)!

Wondering what to do for Dad on Father's Day? Sneak chocolate kisses in his pockets, briefcase, on the dash (Careful! You don't want these things to melt!), next to his shaving gear, or at his work if possible. Wherever Dad will show up during Father's Day week, try to hide a kiss for him. You will have fun, and he will be touched. Well, he'll be *kissed*—over and over again!

50 Percent!

Here's a no-cost gift idea: Give edification, affirmation, and acknowledgment. Paste a note on the fridge that acknowledges something super about a family member.

Try This (for the Bride)!

With a little bit of creativity, you can put together a spice and herb set that any bride will appreciate. Find interesting little bottles or jars, create your own labels, and buy the herbs at the local health food store.

Add to this gift by including a good quality pepper mill. Buy some bulk peppercorns and assemble the box. Throw in loose bay leaves for aroma and presentation.

> *He has showed you, O man, what is good. And what does the LORD require of you? To act justly and to love mercy and to walk humbly with your God.*
>
> MICAH 6:8

Soli Deo Gloria

Epilogue

The Tale of a Better Day

The two of you are warm and comfortable. With sheer grit and willpower, you push yourselves out of bed. This new routine of awakening a half hour earlier has been surprisingly helpful: By taking a brisk walk before your husband jogs, you've benefited with more energy. You also get to listen to the Bible on tape and spend time with your lovable Barky. Hubby has coffee brewing when you get back. He is eternally grateful for the invention of those "gold filters" for the coffee grounds, confessing that he *hated* coping with soggy, day-old filters. He has already steamed broccoli (to add to the egg frittata you will prepare later), taken several slices of whole grain bread from a loaf, and poured the children's orange juice. This is too good to be true! Why did it take the threat of divorce to shake the two of you to your senses? Anyway—you're glad it did. No matter how you got to this place, you like this new arrangement. Forever grateful for your paster's wise counseling, you will never be able to thank him enough.

With barely enough time to bathe before the kids awaken, you use your shower time to pray. This part of your day is dedicated to praise, thanks, and petition. As soon as you are out of the shower, you hear Junior moving around. That means Precious is soon to follow. At this point you are grateful to your *stylist* for your "wash and go" hairstyle!

You give Missy a wake-up call. She has learned you mean business and struggles from bed for fear of the consequence. If she misses the bus, you will no longer be responsible for getting her to school. Amazing that you only had to be good on your threat one time before she got the message.

This is Thursday, which means Junior goes to preschool and Precious goes to your co-op playgroup. (Grateful for *that*, too!) You make a mental note that you're on deck to care for all the kids next Tuesday...or is it Thursday? Better check. The four other women in this arrangement will depend upon you. Your husband has arranged his Tuesday and Thursday work schedule so he can drop off the children. Today he has also agreed to return the videos at the library drive-through. You notice how good he looks in his favorite blue pin-striped permanent press shirt and dark blue tie. You watch bemusedly as he gathers the two young ones to slip on their boots. Precious grabs his finger and walks with him to the car, waddling with boots on the wrong feet.

You have a blessed morning ahead with time to get to your latest editing job. How glad you are to have an outlet for your talents and to have found this telecommuting job! You can easily work two hours before you pick up the kids.

Snacks are due at the preschool meeting. Cream cheese and jam "crackerwiches" on saltines will be easy. You take the cream cheese from the fridge so it will soften. While there, you remove a big tub of frozen chili for dinner, grinning for the coup you pulled on the family: They never detected the chopped spinach you added to this batch! You didn't even get *"What's this green stuff?"* from Missy. You eye a big sack of mini corn on the cob, a favorite with your children and a natural with chili. The veggie bin has lettuce that needs using, so you plan to make a salad. No time to mess with dessert today, so you plan to open a jar of home-canned peaches, compliments of your mother, and make a note to buy real whipped cream.

The children will be hungry when you get them. You slice an apple and put it in a zip-lock baggie. (How did women *live* without these things?!) Whole-wheat Fig Newtons go into their own baggie. Precious gets a sippy cup with milk, and because you want to treat Junior, you add chocolate syrup to milk in his empty water bottle.

At the preschool meeting, you are tempted to volunteer to head a committee, but the job would add too much stress for a mother of three with a part-time job. You tell others that you will help during the fund-raising event itself.

Your drive home from preschool is strategic—you need groceries and gas. The warehouse store is on your route, and now they sell gas. This place takes cash or check only, so you check your wallet. Can't go over $33.29. Not a problem. You need milk, whipped cream, and some produce. Whipped cream comes in a two pack—more than you will use for weeks on end, so you decide to serve the peaches unadorned. And you need dog food. That short-haired mutt of yours from the pound has sure turned out to be a great dog. No upkeep, hardly any shedding, and devoted to the family. You are tempted to buy a seven-dollar sack of rawhide treats for her, but that would cut into your food budget in a big way. Besides, you have a stash of dry dog biscuits at home...not to mention what she manages to beg from the kids.

By the time you get home, Precious has slobbered all over your parka, but it is nothing a wet washcloth can't handle. While she is taking her afternoon nap, Junior has his own quiet time in the dining room. After you haul dry towels straight to the bathroom, you join Junior and work on your project while he plays with his trucks. He interrupts so often that you put aside your work until after dinner and get down on the floor with him. Missy calls for permission to go to a friend's. You are okay with that but want her home by six so you can all eat together.

Barky and Junior play tug-of-war with a wool sock...you wondered where that thing was! Precious awakens, and you decide to take the whole crew for a chilly walk around the block, especially since the sun is shining and you all need a dose of vitamin D.

At four o'clock you turn on PBS Kids and let the children watch two favorite programs. You sit on a big chair with your laptop and get some more work done. (You wonder how on earth women lived without PBS!) The dryer beeps one last time. Since it is a load of children's clothes, you head straight into their room and immediately put the clothes away.

Around five-thirty you put the somewhat frozen chili in a pot on low heat, use a mix to make cornbread, and put a pot of water on the stove so you'll be ready for the corn. You ripped and washed the lettuce last week so you merely decide which salad dressing to use. You shred cheddar for the chili and put out a few extra chunks of cheese for Missy, who is the cheese lover in your family. Alongside the cheese, you put sliced cucumber, cut carrots, and celery chunks filled with peanut butter (a family favorite).

Hubby comes home and plays with the kids for a while before he comes into the kitchen. His job is to get the table ready for dinner and situate the kids in their chairs. Drama Queen Missy arrives with a running commentary on her friend's yucky dinner and grabs a piece of cheese as she announces her science project is due in the morning. You sigh, Hubby chuckles under his breath, and all your plans for work tonight sort of "atomize." After a stern lecture, you join Missy at the kitchen table while Hubby puts the other two in bed.

Late that night you and Hubby discuss finances. Times are tough. You've been whittling that credit card debt down and feel that you are making progress. Selling your somewhat extravagant home and moving into these less expensive digs has made a *huge* difference and taken off a lot of pressure. Before you turn to sleep, the two of you recite the Lord's Prayer and pray for your family. Barky snores loudly under your side of the bed, Junior whimpers in his sleep, and you nestle against your husband's back. *Goodnight, Lord Jesus,* you whisper. *Today has been a good day.* Tomorrow will be even better.

Appendix

Dead Cheese Pie

This uses all the old cheese you have in the refrigerator. It can be savory or sweet, depending on your taste. If you want it to be sweet, add the sweetener of your choice and perhaps raisins, and omit the parsley, onion, and pepper.

2 cups cooked pasta (spaghetti is just fine)

1–2 tablespoons melted butter or olive oil

2 tablespoons dry parsley

1/2 cup chopped onion

4–6 eggs

2 cups old cheese, crumbled or shredded

Salt and pepper

Heat butter or olive oil, sauté onions and parsley, and let cool a bit. Beat eggs in a bowl and add some of the cheese. Then mix everything together and spread into a 9" by 9" pan. Bake 25 minutes at 350 degrees. Cut into squares. Can be served cold. Good for lunches.

Note from me: Please try to cover cheese properly before putting back in the fridge so you don't end up wasting it...even Dead Cheese Pie is not a use for some of those hard, dried-out ends.

The Ten Commandments of Fruitful Living

1. Bring glory to God in thought, word, and deed.

2. Constantly strive to conform to Christ.

3. Invite the Holy Spirit to have His way with you.

4. Constantly hide the Word of God in your heart.

5. Pray specifically.

6. Be certain your response to a person, situation, or issue is godly and not worldly.

7. Ask yourself, *Who is the Christian in this equation?*

8. Be certain your attitude reflects love, joy, and peace.

9. Be certain your behavior reflects patience, kindness, and goodness.

10. Be certain your inner life reflects faithfulness, gentleness, and self-control.

The Creed

I don't want to be a tightwad or a spendthrift.
　　I want to be smart.
I want to celebrate life,
　　to surround myself with beauty,
　　and to be content in whatever state I am in.
I want to manage my finances,
　　to organize my routine,
　　and to use my possessions wisely.
I want to budget resources and time,
　　to help others,
　　and to bring glory to God.

Substitutions

Bread crumbs: Grind up crackers of any kind, or use oatmeal.

Baking chocolate: 3 tablespoons cocoa to 1 tablespoon oil

Heavy cream: 3/4 cup milk to 1/3 cup butter

Light cream: 3/4 cup milk to 3 tablespoons butter

Cake flour: Use regular flour, reduce each cup by two tablespoons, and stir with a whisk to loosen.

Cornstarch: 1 tablespoon cornstarch equals 2 tablespoons flour or 1 1/2 tablespoons instant tapioca

Melted shortening: Use the same amount of oil.

Buttermilk: Add 1 tablespoon vinegar or lemon juice to one cup milk.

Corn syrup: 1/4 cup water and 1 cup sugar

Rum: Use any available juice or flavor extract.

Lemon juice: Use 1/2 teaspoon plain vinegar for every teaspoon lemon juice. Or freeze lemon slices—no bottles, no rotting, no leftover lemons.

Brown sugar: Add 2 tablespoons molasses to 1 cup granulated sugar, mix well.

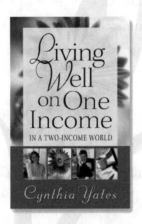